1984

THE IMAGE OF
THE POET

THE IMAGE OF THE POET

British Poets and their Portraits

DAVID PIPER

CLARENDON PRESS · OXFORD
1982

Oxford University Press, Walton Street, Oxford OX2 6DP

London Glasgow New York Toronto
Delhi Bombay Calcutta Madras Karachi
Kuala Lumpur Singapore Hong Kong Tokyo
Nairobi Dar es Salaam Cape Town
Melbourne Auckland
and associates in
Beirut Berlin Ibadan Mexico City Nicosia

Published in the United States
by Oxford University Press, New York

British Library Cataloguing in Publication Data

Piper, David
The image of the poet.
1. Poet in art
I. Title
704.9'423   N8238.P/
ISBN   0−19−817365−2

Set by Macmillan India Ltd
Printed in Great Britain
at the University Press, Oxford
by Eric Buckley.
Printer to the University

In grateful and happy memory of
A. N. L. Munby

Contents

List of Illustrations

This question the Dodo could not answer without a great deal of thought, and it sat for a long time with one finger pressed upon the forehead (the position in which you usually see Shakespeare in pictures of him) while the rest waited in silence.

Alice in Wonderland, LEWIS CARROLL

In speaking of portraits, there is never much to say.

W. M. THACKERAY

1

Shakespeare: 'A Wretched Picture and Worse Bust'

PAUSANIAS recorded statues of the earliest of the great epic poets, Homer and Hesiod, by the temple of Apollo at Olympia. Homer and Hesiod are characters of such antiquity that their identities are hazy in the mists of time, but they are generally believed to have been active in the eighth century BC. By the sixth century BC, poets are both more numerous and a bit more distinct in their biographies. By the fifth century, there is relatively copious evidence that statues to poets were becoming quite frequent in or near Greek temples amongst those of statesmen, philosophers, and other heroes – though the images seem not necessarily to have been very heroic. It is Pausanias Pl. 1 again who records Anacreon, actually on the Acropolis at Athens, 'his posture as it were of a man singing when he is drunk': the connection of alcohol with poets, not unknown today though never an essential characteristic, is established very early.[1]

I mention these very early representations of poets in the hope of establishing at least a venerable respectability for the theme to be discussed in this book. The subject lies on the periphery of literature, and may well seem not merely irrelevant but noxiously distracting, especially to those who distrust any biographical approach to the reading of poetry. To discuss the physical appearance of poets may seem as vain as a discussion of void lobster shells whence the meat has long been abstracted.

My theme, however, will be unashamedly the likenesses of poets, what poets have looked like, what poets have thought they ought to look like, and the not infrequent discrepancy between the two. And what the poets' public or even the public at large have thought poets ought to look like. I say 'theme' but this should not raise expectations that might be disappointed. One of the problems of discussing portraits in any general sense is that a portrait by definition strains away from the general. A likeness of a person shows that he is different from anyone else – excepting always *Doppelgänger* and

2

1 Anacreon (late 6th century BC). Roman copy of a Greek original of *c*.440 BC

identical twins – and a portrait, according to the definition offered by a leading German authority, Delbrück, is the 'representation of a person intended to be like'. To the real portrait enthusiast, to generalize about portraiture is anathema. For the serious historian, on the other hand, portraits are somewhat indigestible: they are not words, nor expressible in words, and so accommodate with difficulty into his exposition and do not fit at all into footnotes. Moreover, they breed irrelevancies: gossip, anecdote, warts and all, flatulence. Even for artists and art historians they present difficulties; in those categories of merit for the various branches of art that theorists used to love to draw up, they tend to get rated very low, if not even actually bottom of the league. This is because portraiture is rooted, more essentially than any other branch of 'fine art', in the faithful imitation of the external appearances of nature. The imitation tends unfortunately quite often to be not merely faithful, but servile. Artists have to earn their bread, and for centuries portraiture was the most stable staple of an artist's livelihood, its drawback being that the client has to like what the artist produces. Hence the temptations to flattery, to an, in fact, disreputably unfaithful interpretation of nature. Portraiture is alas the one form of painting or sculpture in which the artist has a subject which not only can but frequently does argue, and answer back — and not only the subject, but the subject's friends, relations, and, worst of all, wife. When one compromises in art, the results are often artistically mediocre if not downright bad. This I fear is as true of poets' portraiture as of any other kind, while I think few would suggest that a dominant quality in most poets' make-up is modesty, or lack of vanity. Add to that, in an English context, the fact that portraiture was for centuries the most popular form of art — for those who commissioned art, that is — and we have, still hung through the corridors of country houses, a quite remarkable number of very bad pictures.

In face of all that, why bother? My reason is simple. For me this is a reversion to a subject that has fascinated me for very many years. The fascination springs from the fact that, as a lay reader, I have been lit with a more intense delight by poetry than by almost anything else besides great pictures and sculptures, and this delight is followed by wonder that common persons of flesh and blood can be responsible for producing it, and so I want to know what they look like. If they tend to look — as does happen — essentially just like any other individual variation on the human species, that may perhaps be in a way disappointing, but in another way only increases the wonder.

I will not attempt to define my terms very clearly. I have indicated already something of what I mean by 'portrait', although I have not touched on the paradox that sparks some of the greatest portraits in the world: those — and Rembrandt is the great master of them — that transcend the intense particularity of the individual portrayed, while all the time preserving it, into a statement of universal validity and relevance. In front of one of the great Rembrandt self-portraits of his old age, for example — you are looking at him, he is looking at you, yet he is looking at himself, and so you too in him behold yourself. If the painting happens to be glazed, and your own reflection hovers physically between you and the painting, this can lead to actual physical dizziness. But works of art of that quality will not often stop us in our tracks here: Rembrandt was only six years old when Shakespeare died, and the most desirable conjunction of sitter and artist conceivable is inconceivable. Our portraits will be, though of poets, generally more prosaic. As for the poets, I mean simply those who write poems. I will tend naturally to deal with major poets, or at least poets of high distinction, but my coverage will be fairly personal and arbitrary. And the bulk of my illustrations will be confined to English or British poets, *pace* an immigrant or two like Yeats and Eliot. This is primarily a parochial study, and I must leave to others the fascinating task of a more ambitious, international

2 Homer (8th century BC).
Roman copy of a Hellenistic
original

survey, and analysis, perhaps in terms of structuralism or some other ideology.

I would like, though, in turning to the actual images to indicate very briefly the astonishing continuity of the tradition of recording and preserving the images of poets. It does not quite go back to Homer, because in the eighth century BC the convention of naturalistic – or near-naturalistic – portraiture did not exist. Its establishment came about from the fifth to fourth centuries, and it was in the tremendous statue of Mausolus now in the British Museum, about 350 BC, that Roger Hinks diagnosed that 'portraiture, as we understand it, has begun': 'the cast of countenance, the poise of the head, and the whole rhythm of the body, combine to create the impression of a real individual.'[2] Poets appear about that time; thus bronze statues of Aeschylus, Sophocles, Euripides were ordered for the theatre in Athens for the 110th Olympiad, 340 BC. These were all very much posthumous – Aeschylus for example had been dead for a century – but even when posthumous the Hellenistic heads of the great Greek poets and dramatists include images that hold a high place in quality in the history of European portraiture. Even if imaginary, even when known, as most of them are, only through the

3 Euripides (died 406 BC). Roman copy of a Hellenistic orginal

intermediary of late Graeco-Roman or Roman copies, and then generally in the (literally) truncated form of the bust, which the Greeks seem not to have used, they have the most marvellous presence, ideal surely yet held vividly in individuality. Just two examples: a version in the British Museum of the Hellenistic 'blind type' portrait of Homer. This is somewhat restored, but is a fairly lively version of the most widely disseminated type of the four main different types of Homer portraits that survive from antiquity. Rembrandt had a cast of this type,[3] and it is an engraving of a version of it in the Farnese collection that presides as frontispiece over Volume One of Pope's *Iliad* of 1715. More vividly, from the Farnese collection, and now at Naples, comes another bust, again restored but only slightly, and of admirable quality: as the name inscribed indicates, this is Euripides. Both these are as likenesses presumably entirely imaginary, though the Euripides may reflect some tradition going back to his lifetime, and both are, in spite of their individuality, in a sense generic images. They represent men in the reflective wisdom of old age: in general type they do not differ from Greek representations of philosophers or historians, and they clearly represent poets in the capacity of *vates*. The conscience of a people embodied; a distillation in physical form of intellect, imagination, and experience – an admirable equivalent for Shelley's famous assertion of poets as 'the unacknowledged legislators of the world' – though maybe in Athens the moral persuasion of their work was acknowledged more than in Shelley's time or since, while W. H. Auden considered the remark of Shelley (whom he detested) 'the silliest remark ever made about poets'.[4]

As I have noted, these portraits of the Greek poets are known mainly by copies of Roman times or later, and it is quite clear that the Romans did copy them, did collect them, and the number of survivors is impressive. It is indeed startling when one begins to look for contemporary images of the great figures of Latin poetry, for of these there are virtually none at all, at any rate none satisfactorily identified. And that is despite the fact that the Romans quite clearly are rivalled only by the British in their passion for portraiture, and portraiture of the most vividly individualized kind. I have not been able to find any explanation of this extraordinary lack: hardly any historians of classical literature even comment on it, yet one has only to mention the name of Virgil, whose fame never died even through the Dark Ages, to find the failure of any contemporary likeness of him to survive quite baffling. Busts of course are what one would have hoped, indeed expected, to survive; medallic portraiture might also be hoped for: there are some profiles of Greek poets on Greek coins if mostly very late, but the Romans reserved their coin portraiture for emperors, generals, consuls. The other medium, of

Pl. 2

Pl. 3

4 Virgil (70–19 BC).
Mosaic, Roman, 2nd century AD(?)

5 Virgil. From the Vergilius
Romanus, late 5th century
AD

painting, is of course very perishable. Our knowledge of Greek and Roman painted portraiture is virtually nil, but there surely were images of poets, especially in miniature form, as illustration first on scrolls and then on codices or books as we know them now. This is the beginning of the habit of the portrait frontispiece.

Pl. 4   The earliest portrait of Virgil is, though, in mosaic — from the first or second century AD — and is from one point of view disappointing, in that it clearly does not record any tradition of Virgil's physical identity.[5] From another point of view it is very interesting indeed, as, though generic — a poet attended by representatives of the Muses — it shows a basic formula that derives from a Graeco-Roman tradition, notably in reliefs, and will be repeated endlessly in portraiture of literary men in the West. A seated figure with scroll or book contains the essentials to establish a professional identity; a pen, or the presence of a Muse, is more optional. So Virgil appears again, in the earliest surviving book illustration to his works, the Vergilius Pl. 5   Romanus manuscript in the Vatican, of the late fifth century. In scroll form, such illustrations are believed to have been in smaller and medallic format, as the scroll had of course to be rolled; the bound codex permitted a larger, more ambitious design as there was no danger of cracking the portrait by rolling. The Vergilius Romanus image is still relatively constricted, but the formula was soon expanded to full-page scale, and as such survives all through that astounding long abdication from naturalistic representation in art, some six or seven hundred years, of the Dark Ages and the early Middle Ages. Its subject-matter is transformed, and the formula is applied to those founding author-figures of Christianity — Mark, Matthew, Luke, and John. From Constantinople to Lindisfarne it appears again in countless different styles, but the basic formula Pl. 6   remains. In due course, with the Renaissance, the rebirth of lay art, it is reapplied to secular authors and so one finds it in English literature, too, early enough; as, for example, in a frontispiece used for Skelton's poems, about 1545.[6] The medium is that of fairly coarse cutting on Pl. 7   wood, but in it are latent the possibilities of mechanical redupli-cation, opening up rapidly with the increasing sophistication of printing and engraving. It also brings me at last into my English context.

The image of Skelton is of course generic. The professional identification is provided by the pictorial formula, and refined within its category by the laurel worn by the subject and by the inscription: *Poet*. The word *Skelton* is probably the only specific quality of the personal identification — it is very doubtful that there is here an attempt at a physical likeness. In that shortcoming it is a rather archaic image, for the history of the recording of lively likenesses of English poets goes back to well over a century earlier.

The earliest such image is very rightly and properly of the founding father of modern English literature, Geoffrey Chaucer.[7] This image is not only the earliest portrait, in the same sense as we use the word commonly today, in English painting of an English poet: it is just about the first naturalistic portrait, a demonstrable attempt at a likeness, of any Englishman at all, though the likeness of Richard II[8] – as in the Wilton diptych – may be a very few years earlier. Anyway, it is kings, high priests, and poets who first emerge from the faceless Middle Ages. And the intention behind the Chaucer portrait is rather different from that of royal or ecclesiastical ones: all the portraits of Richard II exist still in a religious context – the tomb effigy; the Wilton diptych; the colossal enthroned icon in Westminster Abbey – even though they clearly reflect fairly faithfully the physical identity of a single unique human being. That of Chaucer exists in the context of his work, and of the pious and above all affectionate memory of his colleagues. It is a marvellous *modest* image; and Hoccleve, who had it made some years after Chaucer's death in 1400, spells out the intention in the verses alongside: it is to preserve Chaucer's memory in 'soothfastnesse' lest it fade. The only attribute, other than the modest clothing, seems here to be the rosary, but in a variant of this image, known in various versions, he is shown holding an ink-well or perhaps pen-case at his breast. Further

6 (*left*) St. Mark. From a Carolingian Gospel Book, c.800

7 (*right*) Skelton. Woodcut, from *Certayn Bokes coppied by Mayster Skelton Poet Laureat*, c.1545(?)

Pl. 8

Pl. 9

Hou he þ quaiint was mayden marie
And lat his loue floure and fruntifie

Al þogh his lyfe be queynt þe resemblaunce
Of him hath in me so fressh lyflynesse
Þat to putte othir men in remembraunce
Of his psone I haue heere his lyknesse
Do make to þis ende in sothfastnesse
Þat þei þt haue of him left þought & mynde
By þis peynture may ageyn him fynde

The ymages þt in þe chirche been
Maken folk þenke on god & on his seyntes
Whan þe ymages þei be holden & seen
Were oft vnsyte of hem causith restreyntes
Of þoughtes gode whan a þing depeynt is
Or entailed if men take of it heede
Thoght of þe lyknesse it wil in hym brede

8 (*above*) Chaucer (died 1400). From Hoccleve's *De Regimine Principum*, early 15th century AD

9 (*right*) Chaucer. (?)late 16th century

elaboration can easily creep in; thus, in a little whole-length derivation, posterity has succumbed to one of the abiding temptations of the portrait: to use it as a statement or identification of social status, and his heraldic arms are added in.[9] By about 1600, versions in oil were being produced.[10]

The only surviving portrait of Chaucer's very different contemporary, John Gower, who died in 1408, seems at first sight almost entirely an identification of social status, and is not one bit modest. His tomb (in Southwark Cathedral) is now dazzlingly polychrome after restoration, and what relation to his features the effigy's face may bear is all the more speculative; the pretensions, though, are very clear, and Gower lies in splendour, in his gorgeous gown with the gold chain given him by the King, and his arms fully emblazoned. Yet he is in fact identified as poet — his head rests, not   Pl. 10 on a helmet or a pillow, but a pile of three of his books, and in all three of the languages in which he wrote — Latin, French, and English.[11] His bets are hedged as to which language will be the safest medium for the preservation of his fame for posterity, but English is at least one of them. Chaucer (and Hoccleve) had no such doubts, and it is right that the national shrine of poets' memory, Poets' Corner in Westminster Abbey, should have grown up around Chaucer's tomb and not Gower's at Southwark; though Chaucer's tomb has no effigy at all, his heirs would certainly be provided with them.

That was to take some time. The habit of portraiture was relatively slow to establish itself in England — hardly any portraits other than tomb effigies survive from the fifteenth century — and although, with Holbein's performance first in Thomas More's circle and later at Henry VIII's court, the full possibilities of the painted portrait were demonstrated, and with a quality that has never been surpassed, it was not until the end of the sixteenth century that the practice of getting oneself painted spread outside court circles. One Holbein image of the poet Wyatt, near-profile in the classicizing   Pl. 11 tradition of the Renaissance, does indeed have poetic overtones, but all Surrey's portraits show him as courtier and aristocrat.[12]

By Shakespeare's time the situation had changed, but even so the existence of a portrait then most often is evidence that its subject was of the upper, landed, and propertied classes. There are of course exceptions — a notable one is recorded in the earliest full autobiography in English, by the musician Whythorne, who sat for his portrait no less than three times in the third quarter of the sixteenth century.[13] But the lack of portraits of poets when one starts looking for them is fairly complete. Nothing certain of Spenser even, for all his court connections and his fame; nothing of Marlowe except the splendid, frequently reproduced but entirely speculatively identified one discovered lurking at Corpus Christi College, Cambridge, a few

10 Gower. Effigy, c.1408

years ago. Nothing of any of the so-called University Wits. And so on. It would not then be surprising if there were nothing at all of Shakespeare himself, and the fact that there are two portraits, posthumous but both done, like the Chaucer, within a few years – seven at most, to be exact – of his death, has to be regarded as a bonus; while the existence of a third, a painting of reasonable professional competence from the life, that retains a very strong, if unproven, possibility of being an authentic likeness, is even more so.

Unhappily all these three, but especially the two authenticated ones, cannot be claimed as more than average in quality – of the two, one is incompetently drawn, and the other is a vapid icon. Both, if they did not happen to represent Shakespeare, would have receded into oblivion almost instantaneously. On the other hand, while the discrepancy between their quality and that of the genius they celebrate, or at least record, has distressed posterity, it gives posterity all the sharper spur to reconstitute Shakespeare into a shape more worthy of himself. So that succeeding generations have tended to re-create Shakespeare, and their re-creations tend also to be very much in their own image: Shakespeare becomes in a sense an ever-changing embodiment of the *Zeitgeist*. This process will provide a continuing theme of reference for me, and it moves in approximate parallel of course with the progress of reinterpretation of his actual work. I will also be glancing from time to time at the progress of subsidiary motifs in this theme – its interpretation and application in the shape of the prone, or prostrate, poet, of which Gower was the first example, as also in the shape of the cross-legged or leaning, melancholic standing figure, which comes rather later.

I must now remind the reader of the two authentic images. Reminding may seem gratuitous, as they are two of the most

11 Wyatt. After Holbein: from Leland's *Noenia*, 1548

Pl. 12

insistently reproduced, not to say hackneyed, images in the whole English repertoire. One is the engraving, signed in the plate by one Martin Droeshout. The other is the bust, in Shakespeare's parish church at Stratford-upon-Avon, incorporated in his monument in the wall over his grave.[14] The claim for authenticity of these two images rests in the fact that both are vouched for implicitly in the First Folio, published seven years after Shakespeare's death, in 1623. The engraving is of course the frontispiece itself, while the existence of the bust in the church is referred to in one of the celebratory poems, that by Leonard Digges, that preface the plays. The editors of the Folio were Shakespeare's colleagues and friends: those responsible for the erection of the bust must likewise have been his friends and his family. Both images were therefore, even if both were made posthumously, vouched for, passed for publication as likenesses of Shakespeare by those who knew him — accepted or, at least, not rejected by them.

Both, however, present problems. The notorious incompetence of the engraving has led to incredulous dismay that any engraver of such lack of skill should have been entrusted with the definitive image of a man frequently described as the greatest Englishman in history. Droeshout was of an immigrant Anglo-Netherlandish dynasty of craftsmen but only twenty or so when this engraving was done; he was born in 1601, and so only fifteen when Shakespeare died. He must have been at this point a craftsman of limited experience; his work in fact was never to be prolific, yet the rest of it is surely of superior quality to this. The oddities of the image, the apparent possession by the sitter of two left (or right) shoulders rather than a left and a right one, has led to many ingenious, often cabbalistic and highly perverse interpretations of it, which can be studied in the weird literature of pamphlet and counter-pamphlet that has grown up around it. I would only observe, first, that there were two Martin Droeshouts: an uncle, and a nephew; virtually nothing is known about the uncle, but I sometimes wonder if this engraving may not be his work rather than his nephew's. Second — and this suggestion applies equally well to the bust at Stratford — that if the renderings of the likeness are very unsubtle, it may be rash to base subtle arguments on them. The print is, however, almost certainly a transposition of a portrait in another medium into engraving: the original, lost of course, could have been a drawing or a painting, and could have been done from memory or from life. It has been suggested that it would have been a miniature in the manner of Nicholas Hilliard, but the evident lack of modelling by light and shade was common to much of both miniature and life-scale painting of the period. The costume is of 1610, give or take five years or so either side. The mode of presentation here for a frontispiece is not

Mr. WILLIAM

SHAKESPEARES

COMEDIES,
HISTORIES, &
TRAGEDIES.

Published according to the True Originall Copies.

Martin Droeshout sculpsit London.

LONDON
Printed by Isaac Iaggard, and Ed. Blount. 1623.

12 Shakespeare. By M. Droeshout, before 1623

13 Shakespeare. By G. Johnson, before 1623

14 John Stow. By Nicholas Johnson, 1605

only rather clumsy, but already old-fashioned, even though by 1623 the portrait frontispiece was still something of a novelty. In contrast, the image of George Chapman, translator of Homer, besides being far more accomplished in technique, is in a far more sophisticated mode, yet is earlier (1616) than the Shakespeare, and published within the author's lifetime, unlike the Shakespeare.[15] It is also rather pretentious, that head within clouds with symbolic or emblematic overtones, underlining the fact that the Shakespeare was surely intended by his friends in exactly the same modest and affectionate spirit as that in which Hoccleve had Chaucer's image made.

Now, however, for the bust. It was erected by 1623, and carved by, again, a member of an Anglo-Dutch craftsman dynasty, based in Southwark, Gerard Johnson. It is not signed, but the name of the sculptor was recorded by Dugdale about 1655, and fits stylistically. But, also again, there were two Gerard Johnsons, and this must be the younger one, who was alas also the weakest of the clan in ability.[16] Apart from the attempt at likeness, it is an exercise in a standard monumental convention, and repeats more or less verbatim, though showing less of the figure, the formula by Gerard's brother, Nicholas, for the antiquarian and chronicler, John Stow, set up in St.

Pl. 13

Pl. 14

Andrew Undershaft in London in 1605, which is more lively. While it is interesting that a formula usually applied to scholar or divine has been used, and the quill specifically perpetuated in the sitter's right hand, I feel the major intention was more towards a social identification, while his coat of arms is included, relatively large, in the monument. Even though the inscription, like the pen, indicates his profession, this is basically the effigy of a respectable and respected, well-to-do burgher of this small market town. It is respectable indeed to the point of tedium, the quill through which that extraordinary genius found its expression seeming slightly frivolous or anyway light-weight (though it was apparently originally of stone, but 'dropped and broken by a young gentleman from Oxford' some time before 1827).[17] It is a portrait of a gentleman, an armigerous gentleman of standing, who from time to time, as George III noted of Gibbon, fancied scribbling. As in the case of the print, countless doubts have been raised about this image. Is it the one that was originally put up or is it a substitution? What relation does it bear to its original? And so on. I can accept it perfectly happily as being a representation of the same man that the engraving represents, though obviously based on a different though equally lost original of him, which again may or may not have been posthumous. The present colours (eyes brown gone dark, doublet red, gown black) have to be seen with some caution – as will emerge later, they have been renewed not once but several times. The carving may have been a bit earlier than the engraving; the near-by tomb of John Combe is also ascribed to Gerard Johnson, and Combe who died in 1614 left provision for the erection of his tomb within a year of his death. If advantage was taken of the sculptor visiting Stratford to do Shakespeare as well, that could bring the monument to a date very close to his death (and actually not impossibly before it).

However, it is safest to proceed on the assumption that both engraving and monument are posthumous, though they have marked physical traits in common – notably that idiosyncratic dome of a head – enough to suggest that there is no reason why they should not reflect, at some distance and by different media, the same original of flesh and blood. The third image however has all the signs of having been done direct from the life – the painting known as the

Pl. 15

Chandos portrait. By gift of this, in 1856, the Earl of Ellesmere founded the collections of the National Portrait Gallery and it is number one on the Gallery's register. This, though the artist is unknown, is of professional quality if of not more than average competence; technically, it is entirely compatible – in materials used, as in style and handling – with a date in the second decade of the seventeenth century, or even the first decade. The costume fits a similar date and has nothing unusual, other than the gold ear-ring,

15 Shakespeare. The
'Chandos' portrait

16 Shakespeare. The
'Chandos' portrait, infra-red
photograph

which adds a slight panache to this otherwise modest image but was a not uncommon accessory of masculine dress. The handling, though not especially lively, does not suggest the work of a copyist, but rather that of an artist working from the life. The whole surface is rather rubbed, and restored in places, but the image now visible is probably close enough to what it was in its mint state to retain a degree of faithfulness to its sitter's appearance. Overpaint, as can be seen clearly in the infra-red photograph, has slightly toned down the uncompromising loft of the dome so marked in the other two portraits. So far, then, so good: the problem that remains, and is likely to remain for ever unproven, one way or the other, is whether its sitter was Shakespeare or some other contemporary who shared some physical features with him. I cannot go into the complex pedigree of the painting here, but the essential facts are that in 1719 it certainly belonged to one Robert Keck, who claimed that it had come, via the great leading actor Betterton (whom Keck surely knew), from the playwright and styled Poet Laureate, Sir William Davenant. Betterton died in 1710; Davenant, for whom Betterton had worked, in 1668, and Davenant claimed either — depending I think on how drunk he was — that he was Shakespeare's godson, or not merely that, but Shakespeare's illegitimate offspring. It brings us anyway within living memory of the poet, while Davenant is agreed, as a recent biographer says, to have been regarded 'as the repository of a greater and more authentic mass of Shakespeariana than any other living man'. The trouble is that Davenant is also clearly a very unreliable witness: a character of considerable huff and puff, much given to romanticizing. I believe the painting is of Shakespeare, but it is only a belief which, though it has circumstantial evidence in its favour, cannot be considered in any way proven. What is certain is that well before the end of the seventeenth century it was accepted as Shakespeare, but to that we shall come later.

Taken out of its context, the specific function for which any portrait was made, its occasion, is usually, rather than unusually, very difficult if not impossible to establish. In Shakespeare's case, that of the two certain images is straightforward. Both are in context still, exercises in an established and continuing tradition. The engraving of a frontispiece was becoming, by the time of the First Folio of 1623, a quite usual embellishment: a tradition reaching back to the scrolls and codices of antiquity, and basically arising from the fact that the author is talking to you. The printed word is the spoken word materialized: if someone talks to you, you turn to the speaker to see who it is, and so when reading his words you turn equally naturally to the portrait frontispiece to see who is addressing you. Technically, of course, the convention became widely, indeed universally, established when printing and the craft of the metal engraver jointly were developed enough to accommodate illustrations in mass-produced books. The Droeshout engraving is an identification of its subject in terms of that convention, though but a very mediocre specimen of it. The Stratford bust is of course likewise an exercise but in a considerably more solidly established tradition, the tomb monument in a church, and it is a memorial summary of a worthy citizen who is now dead. The painting, however, seems essentially a personal or private identification rather than a public one, and we have no clue as to why it should have been made. It could have been for any or several of the many reasons for which portraits did and still do get painted: as status symbol, a narcissistic part of domestic furniture for a prosperous householder, or perhaps by way of keeping up with the Joneses. Samuel Pepys had his own portrait painted in part for just those reasons fifty years later. Then there are the factors of simple vanity, or, more attractively, of the need of someone who loves the portrait's subject, or of an institution that he has served, perhaps as benefactor, to have his image; more casually, a chance meeting with a painter looking for work. More essentially, a need, deeper than mere vanity, on the part of the sitter to reject annihilation by death, though that is of course itself a vanity of vanities, and certain limited immortality – if I may use such a phrase – is far better ensured by the word which, as Shakespeare noted, endures better:

> Not marble, nor the gilded monuments
> Of princes, shall outlive this powerful rime . . .

A sentiment taken up by the young Milton, in his sonnet for Shakespeare, that appeared first in the Second Folio of 1632, a mere sixteen years after Shakespeare's death:

> What needs my Shakespeare for his honour'd Bones,
> The labour of an age in piled Stones . . .
> Dear son of Memory, great heir of Fame,
> What need'st thou such weak witness of thy name?
> Hast built thyself a live-long Monument . . .

I suspect Shakespeare would have agreed, but posterity has not.

Before contemplating Milton himself, first and perhaps greatest in the galaxy of Cambridge poets, I must glance at other possible modes of identification by portrait that one might have hoped to find in Shakespeare's case according to the fashion of his times. Portrait painters, from Holbein to Romney and beyond, have been praised by poets for their ability to catch the soul within the face; to create, while recording a physical likeness, an all-round and in-depth character, of the inner man no less than the outer man: in short, to contain the essential biography within the physical likeness. Nowadays, a cliché often applied to successful portrait painters is to praise their 'psychological insight'. In fact, of course, the artist cannot spell out and analyse qualities of mind and spirit in his sitter as can a biographer: his methods of characterization of anything other than the outer man are generally not very subtle. He can do it by inserting attributes — coats of arms, pens for writers, books, and so on — to indicate certain fairly broad categories to which his subject belongs. A heraldic identification in some Elizabethan paintings can seem indeed to take over entirely, the coat of arms emblazoned demanding more attention than the face, and the stiff, shadowless style of the painters seeming to demonstrate the sitter as a heraldic supporter, supporting for the time being the pride and virtue of the family. There are, however, literary modes of characterization well established in Shakespeare's time for which one might seek hopefully for visual equivalents. There was the medieval tradition of analysing plus creating character in terms of allegory, of a conflict of virtues

17 Henry Percy, 9th Earl of Northumberland. By Nicholas Hilliard, *c.*1590

and vices; there was the more symbolic – and by 1600 highly fashionable – technique of describing characters in terms of emblems, devices, conceits. These were often essentially visual, and frequently enough emblems are indeed built into Elizabethan portraits, while by 1645 the French emblematic writer Estienne could claim that the emblem or device could almost replace or supersede the conventional portrait of the outer man. Painting, he said, could only represent 'the body and exquisite features of the face, whereas a Device exposeth the rare conceipts and gallant resolutions of its author with far more perspicuity'.[18]

The artist who most famously drew on these ideas in his portraits was the miniaturist Nicholas Hilliard, but normally he used a very mixed method, combining what was evidently a very remarkable skill in catching the individual physical likeness with a build–up of inner character by the use of inscriptions, devices, emblems, symbolic happenings. It would be delightful to have a Shakespeare by Hilliard in such fashion, and recently, indeed, the ingenious Dr Hotson has demonstrated to his own satisfaction that we and he do indeed have one: to that I will return later,[19] and I would only comment at this juncture that Dr Hotson's feeling that there ought to be such a portrait is more convincing than his demonstration that one actually exists. A richer example of Hilliard's symbolic style is offered by his whole-length of a young man, melancholy and prone

Pl. 17

18 Lord Herbert of Cherbury. By Isaac Oliver, *c.*1610(?)

with his book; he lies in rather angular repose in a close-walled garden with orderly trees, set in a wild landscape. Suspended from a tree, it seems almost in defiant anticipation of Calder mobiles, a globe or cannon-ball balances exactly a feather or quill, with the word TANTI floating effortlessly below. One message of this enigmatic imagery is perhaps that the power of the pen can equate almost any other power. The sitter is probably Henry, 9th Earl of Northumberland, better known as the 'Wizard Earl' owing to his penchant for alchemical and other investigations, but here in a most poetic characterization.[20] The portrait of Lord Herbert of Cherbury — who was of course amongst the most interesting of the 'metaphysical' poets — is specifically poetic.[21] It is another exercise in the prone portrait, by Hilliard's successor in fashion, Isaac Oliver; Oliver worked in the more up-to-date, softer, and naturalistic manner of the Flemish painters, but is also here continuing the somewhat archaicizing, medievalizing tradition of Elizabethan chivalry and romance. The subject is a knight, ready — though not yet in armour — for the tilt in which he will be defending his lady's honour: his shield bears an emblem, and the painting is inscribed *Magica Sympathiae*.

Pl. 18

Of Herbert, whose vanity both introspective and highly extrovert is witnessed in his famous *Autobiography*, the braggadocio of an almost Baron Munchausen figure, there have survived a number of interestingly various portraits. These have in common strong implicit suggestions that they were composed to his own programmes, and indicate for the first time a considerable measure of conscious attempt by a poet to present a controlled image of himself to the world.[22] From this aspect, the case of Dr John Donne is even more interesting.[23] The earliest portrait of Donne is of 1591, when he was only eighteen years old: it dates from those shadowy years, 1589–91, during which his life is very obscure; he had been both at Oxford (certainly) and, according to Walton, at Cambridge, but those two years before he entered the Inns of Court in 1592 are virtually a blank, one of the few points of reference in which is this portrait. Its occasion, though, is entirely unknown: it is often suggested that its original was a miniature by Hilliard, perhaps more on the strength of Donne's endlessly quoted reference to Hilliard ('. . . a hand, or eye / By *Hilliard* drawne, is worth an history, / By a worse painter made') rather than owing to any specific quality in the portrait in the form in which it is now known. That is, in an engraving by William Marshall, used first for the 1635 edition of Donne's *Poems*. The original itself could have been miniature or life-scale, but surely in the shadowless, linear style of which Hilliard was the greatest exponent. The engraving gives age and date, indicates that the boy is armigerous, and shows him clearly as a young spark of high fashion: elegantly clad, ear-ringed, one slender hand on the

Pl. 19

ANNO. DNI. 1591.   ANTES MVDADO
ÆTATIS SVÆ:18   MVERTO QVE

This was for youth, Strength, Mirth, and wit that Time
Most count their golden Age; but t'was not thine.
Thine was thy later yeares, so much refind
From youths Drosse, Mirth, & wit; as thy pure mind
Thought (like the Angels) nothing but the Praise
Of thy Creator, in those last, best Dayes.
Witnes this Booke, (thy Embleme) which begins
With Love; but endes, with Sighes, & Teares for sins.

Will: Marshall sculpsit.   IZ:WA:

19 Donne. By William
Marshall, from a lost portrait of 1591, in the *Poems*,
1635

sword, hair fashionably long. That this is a true impression is
supported by Izaak Walton's verses inscribed under the print, even
though the lines are of around 1635, after Donne's death, and not
contemporary with the original: 'This was for youth, Strength,
Mirth and wit that Time / Most count their Golden Age; but 't was
not thine / thine was thy later yeares . . .' — the later years when
Donne's genius had turned to religion. The second portrait is
generally dated about 1595; it is surely not much earlier but could be
much later, as late as his secret marriage in 1609, or even after that. It
is a portrait very much 'in character', and Donne has adopted the

20 Donne. By an unknown
artist, c.1595(?)

Pl. 20

posture and dress of melancholic love; it is inscribed, in parody of the
Psalms, with a Latin inscription to his love: *Illumina tenebras nostras
domina*. Though his later pleas for light in darkness were addressed to
a higher source, this portrait of himself was in his possession when he
died and was left in his Will — *that picture of mine which is taken in the
shadows* — to Robert Kerr, Earl of Ancrum. For years it was believed
lost, until Mr John Bryson, seeing no reason why it should not still be
with Robert Kerr's descendants, the Marquesses Lothian, probed
deeper. So in 1959 it was rediscovered, it is said in a Lothian
housemaid's cupboard and having got mislabelled as Duns Scotus:[24]
a not untypical, if spectacular, example of the way portraits can get
lost and wrongly identified.

That is a portrait in as remarkable a strain of poetic melancholy as
any young poet could wish. The next one is in purely private
character: it dates from about the time of Donne's ordination, a

miniature in modest, intimate format, but brilliantly executed by
Isaac Oliver, who signed and dated it 1616. Its occasion is unknown,   Pl. 22
but its identification as Donne is secured by its 'going public' in
engraved form, for the posthumous publication of *LXXX Sermons* in   Pl. 21
1640; there it is transposed from miniature to funerary monumental
key. The fourth portrait is again strange and unusual in mood as in
mode: a circular painting of which versions are in the Deanery in St.
Paul's and in the Victoria and Albert Museum. It is dated 1620, at the   Pl. 23
time of, or shortly before, Donne's becoming Dean, but shows him
in classical garb, not ecclesiastical. It is a strange echo, transmitted
through I do not know what intermediaries, of the form of classical
author-image of early codices, such as that of Terence in a ninth-
century manuscript in the Vatican, which doubtless reflects a much

22 (*above*) Donne.
Miniature, by Isaac Oliver,
1616

21 (*left*) Donne. Engraving,
by M. Merian, after Oliver,
from *LXXX Sermons*, 1640

23 Donne. Artist unknown, 1620

Pl. 25

earlier original, and relates likewise to medallion reliefs on Roman sarcophagi. It is, however, reminiscent of Holbein's woodcut of Thomas Wyatt, though that shows its subject, almost in profile, eyes cast upwards, in style closer to the classical medallic formula popular in the Renaissance. Its purpose is lost, but its identification is again assured by its publication in engraved form, by P. Lombart, as

Pl. 24

frontispiece to the 1651 edition of the *Letters*. All these, other than the Oliver miniature, are out of line with the ordinary portraits of the time, and have a marked element of role-playing, but none so much as the last, most extraordinary and famous of them all: the upright shrouded effigy in St. Paul's Cathedral.

No less famous than the monument itself is Izaak Walton's account of its begetting, one act in Donne's inspired but severely controlled performance (at least, as it is reported by Izaak Walton) of his own dying through the last month of his life, March 1631. Donne, persuaded by Simon Fox that there ought to be a monument over his grave, sat or rather stood for it. Naked within his shroud, he stood in his study, on a model of the urn, his face to the east, his eyes closed, while a charcoal fire burned, and an unnamed artist drew him

24 Donne. Engraving, by P. Lombart, from the *Letters*, 1651

25 Terence. Illumination, 9th century AD

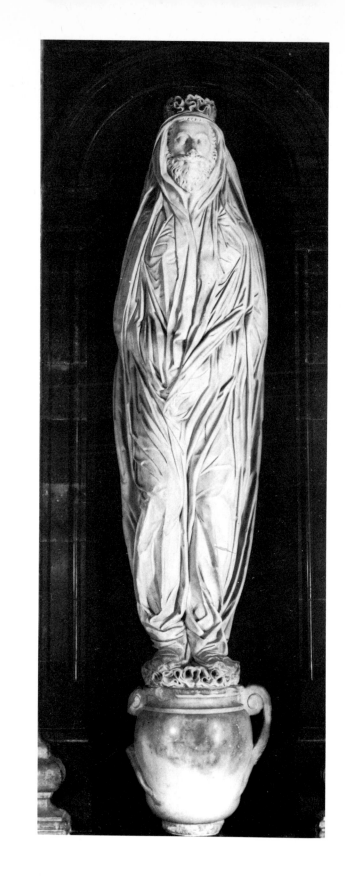

thus life-size on a wooden plank. A record of the upper part of that drawing or painting, itself lost, seems to be provided by an engraver we have met before – Martin Droeshout – as frontispiece to Donne's last sermon, *Death's Duell*, published probably early in 1632. The monument carved by Nicholas Stone and his workshop, from the design recorded by the now-lost drawing, is extraordinary enough, but the folds of the shroud show that the carvers were unwilling to stretch their imaginations to the concept of an upright shrouded figure. The engraving suggests that the drawing showed the drapery falling vertically, as one would expect, but on the effigy itself it settles against the body as it would on a recumbent figure, and it detracts perhaps a little from the flame-like originality of its conception. Though the eyes be closed still, it speaks of course of Resurrection. 'I am full', said Donne, 'of unexpressible joy, and shall dye in peace.' Some especial providence presided over the effigy too, and its survival, when old St. Paul's burned in the great fire of 1666, is itself almost miraculous. Even though recent enquiry[25] has raised well-argued and sadly credible scepticism about the accuracy of Walton's account of the coming into being of this image, it remains one of the most haunting of English effigies.

27 (*left*) Donne. By Nicholas Stone (detail)

28 (*right*) Donne. Engraving, by M. Droeshout, from *Death's Duell*, 1632

Donne's portraits offer a most unusually rich and illuminating commentary on his life, and his own sensitivity to the visual arts must have been in no small part responsible. Like his old friend, Henry Wotton, he was a connoisseur and a collector. Milton, even before blindness overtook him, seems to have confined his very remarkable imagery to language, even though telling parallels can be made, and have been made, with his verbalized imagery and that in the paint of an artist such as Poussin. His portraiture[26] is disappointing: as with Donne, there are five certain portrait types, of which three are of the private kind, and two public. He was in fact painted at an even earlier age than Donne – aged ten, a tidy and inexpressive child – by an unknown painter and now in The Pierpont Morgan Library, New York; then again, when he was about twenty-one and a student at Christ's College ('he was so faire yt. they called him Lady of Xts. Coll;' – according to Aubrey), now in the National Portrait Gallery. These are generally agreed to be identical with two paintings described by Aubrey about 1681 when they were in the possession of Milton's widow. On the other hand, the most recent study[27] in detail of Milton's portraits points out, with what seems to me a rather exaggerated scepticism, that it is very far from being *proved* that this is so. The sceptic (Leo Miller) is also sceptical about the third, the

Pl. 29

Pl. 30

29 Milton. Aged 10, artist unknown

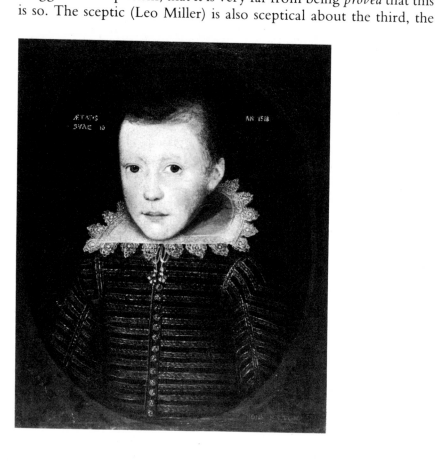

30 Milton. The 'Onslow portrait', *c.*1629

head in unbaked clay now in Christ's College. All three were accepted as being of Milton quite early in the eighteenth century, and I would rather accept the tradition of identification if the evidence for abandoning it is inconclusive. The first two, besides being fascinating items for the contemplation of pious sentiment, are likely to be witness of parental love and pride by the young prodigy's father and mother: they both evidently remained in the poet's possession. The third, the clay head, is unexplained. While there is no reason to think it was not modelled from the life, there is nothing of the period quite like it; its purpose and occasion are obscure, and it could be later than the date of 1650 or so that costume and apparent age suggest. Pl. 31

The remaining two portraits both became public property in Milton's lifetime. The first, engraved by that William Marshall who had engraved the early portrait of Donne, appears as frontispiece to Milton's *Poems* of 1645. This seems straightforward: the poet set Pl. 32 amongst the Muses, with a sturdy bucolic jive going on in the

31 Milton. Clay, unbaked

background. Closer inspection breeds problems. The Latin inscription round the oval gives: 'Portrait of John Milton Englishman in the 21st year of his age.' Milton, by 1645, was of course around 37 rather than 20/21. The younger age fits the poems in the book, which are all juvenilia written before he was 21; the older age seems to fit the face better (certainly so if the painting of him as student is rightly named), as does the costume which is surely nearer 1645 than 1628. Various factors lead me to a guess (it is not much more than a guess though it does reconcile the discrepancies in the engraving): it is that a portrait of Milton at about 20 was intended to be the original, and the framework of the design was so made; then, such a portrait being for some reason unavailable, Milton was drawn from the life in 1644 or 1645. What seems certain is that Milton disapproved, letting it go

Melpo'mene.   Erato.

IOANNIS MILTONI ANGLI EFFIGIES ANNO ÆTATIS VIGeß: Pri:·

Urania.   Clio

Ἀμαθεῖ γεγράφθαι χειρὶ τήνδε μὲν εἰκόνα
Φαίης τάχ' ἄν, πρὸς εἶδος αὐτοφυὲς βλέπων·
Τὸν δ' ἐκτυπωτὸν ὀκ ἐπιγνόντες φίλοι
Γελᾶτε φαύλου δυσμίμημα ζωγράφου.
W·M· *sculp:*

32 Milton. By William
Marshall, from the *Poems*,
1645

forward but with the Greek inscription at the bottom. This is
evidently by himself, and was obligingly copied on to the plate by
the engraver. The engraver evidently did not understand Greek, or
was a very meek and mild character, as the Greek, though somewhat
convoluted, is clear in that it derides both the quality of the engraver
and that of the image as a likeness of the sitter. I cannot, though, go
along with Mr Leo Miller in his suggestion that Marshall's image was
intended as something of a caricature, to show Milton as 'an oddball
heretic'. As a Miltonic joke, it is anyway on the heavy side, but while
it demonstrates that the convention of the portrait frontispiece is a
firmly enough established convention for it to be played about with,
it also suggests that as a likeness of Milton, it should be viewed with
some reservations: elsewhere Milton says it is 'most unlike me'.

Gul. Faithorne ad Vivum   *Delin. et sculpsit.*

Joannis Miltoni Effigies Ætat: 62.
1670.

33 Milton. By William
Faithorne, 1670

Pl. 33

The last image of all, the one by which Milton is known wherever
he is read, is that by the draughtsman-engraver William Faithorne: a
crayon drawing which may be the original of this is at Princeton, but
it was broadcast by Faithorne's engraving of it, dated and signed as *ad
vivum*: 1670, Milton's age 62. This was first published in the *History
of Britain* of 1670, and subsequently endlessly copied.[28] It is certainly,
as the antiquary George Vertue noted about 1730, 'The most
authentic likeness'. It gives, though, no indication of Milton's
blindness, and is set within an entirely conventional framework,
with no allegorical trimmings, just, as it were, the equivalent in
engraving of the sculpted memorial bust in its niche; a formula that
repeats for the next two hundred years for hundreds of authors in
their frontispieces, varying only in details of dress, inscription, but
with of course each one individualized by the sitter's own face.

Milton had doubted Shakespeare's need of any monument, and no doubt he felt the same about one for himself. Meanwhile, Shakespeare's own image remained fairly quiescent. Stratford had yet to become the most-visited tourist attraction in England outside London; in fact, it was still a remote market town, a day or even several days from the capital. The only publication of the bust before the end of the century was in an engraving in Dugdale's *Antiquities of Warwickshire*, 1656. We are indebted to Dugdale in that it was he who recorded the sculptor's name, but there indebtedness ceases, for the transcription of the appearance of the monument is so misleading as to be almost libellous. This was but the first of many outrages the bust was to suffer. Dugdale's interest was not in Shakespeare as poet, or even as individual human being, but as the bearer of a certain coat of arms: Dugdale was a professional herald, and the original drawing, previously unpublished, in his manuscript of the book underlines the point.[29] What interested him was neither the sculpture nor the man, but the coat of arms. Otherwise, the main source for those who wanted to know what Shakespeare looked like was the Folios: the First of 1623; the Second, 1632; the Third, 1663–4; and Fourth and Last in 1685. In all four the Droeshout engraving was reprinted from its original plate, but by the last this had become much worn and had to be heavily (and rather coarsely) retouched.

Pl. 34

Pl. 35

34 (*left*) Shakespeare. From Dugdale's *Antiquities of Warwickshire*, 1656

35 (*right*) Shakespeare. From the MS of Dugdale's *Antiquities of Warwickshire*, 1656

The only two variations of it of any substance and interest in the seventeeth century were those by Marshall – the engraver also of Donne and of Milton – and Faithorne. The Marshall image,[30] frontispiece to the 1640 edition of the *Poems*, tidies up the anatomical difficulties of the Droeshout by hanging a cloak on one shoulder; he endows Shakespeare with a rather prim and pursed elegance, but does provide him with a hand and a poet's bays for it to clutch. The engraving ascribed to Faithorne, used for the *Rape of Lucrece* in its 1655 edition, is mainly concerned with the pathos of Lucretia, but insets a very much cheered-up version of Droeshout's image of the poet himself.

Pl. 37

That is almost all that there is of Shakespeare through the seventeenth century. As far as images of him were concerned, Shakespeare might have agreed with Byron, who in *Don Juan* inquired cynically about the end of Fame, and found it was 'To have, when the original is dust, / A wretched picture and worse bust'. Yet there were some signs. An early and enchanting tribute was registered by no less than Van Dyck in the late 1630s at the behest of Sir John Suckling:[31] Shakespeare himself does not appear, but Suckling is shown in an Arcadian setting, reading *Hamlet*. The pose is

36 (*left*) Shakespeare. By W Marshall after Droeshout, from the *Poems*, 1640

37 (*right*) Shakespeare. By W. Faithorne after Droeshout, from *The Rape of Lucrece*, 1655

38 Suckling. By Van Dyck, c.1637(?)

40

39 (*right*) Shakespeare. By
Gerard Soest, *c.*1650–60(?)

40 (*below*) 'The Inspiration
of the Artist'. By Gerard
Soest

unlikely and few would choose to read the First or Second Folio standing up and out of doors, but at least Suckling and Shakespeare are celebrated in painting of high quality. And also the more ambitious portraits of Shakespeare begin to appear, like a somewhat mysterious one now at Stratford-upon-Avon.[32] It is by a painter of competence called Gerard Soest and relates, if not quite in all probability nevertheless in reasonable likelihood, to a story that was recorded early in the next century of such a portrait being painted of an actor who was said to resemble Shakespeare very closely — it is in fact of about 1650, clearly of a living person but dressed in a partial attempt at costume of thirty or forty years earlier. There is here perhaps a tradition, still in the living memory of the mid seventeenth century, of Shakespeare's appearance. The same painter, Soest, also produced a remarkable painting that seems relevant. Its title is lost, but it could well be, if not a specific portrait, a romantic personification of the poetic imagination in reverie, the baroque equivalent of those prone whole-lengths by Hilliard and Oliver.

The modest Soest painting of the actor dressed as Shakespeare, if it indeed be that, may also be a symptom of dissatisfaction with the

Pl. 39

Pl. 40

41 Shakespeare. By P. Borsseler(?), *c.*1660–70 (The 'Chesterfield portrait')

Pl. 41

portraits available. Further evidence of that comes, about 1660–70, in the first transposition into grander key of the third portrait of Shakespeare, the painting called the Chandos portrait. This is of about 1660–70 and the head is clearly based on the Chandos portrait (and is incidentally the earliest solid evidence of identification of the Chandos portrait as Shakespeare). It has been attributed to a Dutch painter called Borsseler, active in England in the 1660s, but, whether by him or not, it is an exercise in the full-blown baroque manner of Van Dyck. This is surely how Davenant would see Shakespeare, as fitting author for those plays which Davenant after the Restoration was revising and re-staging in operatic or near-operatic form: an amply generous figure, shown with one hand flung on the open Folio, the other extended in rhetoric. Later, it belonged to the Earl of Chesterfield, and hung in the place of honour over the fireplace, central in a galaxy of poets' portraits over the shelves of his library.[33] This is the beginning of a long sequence of variations and modulations on the theme of the Chandos portrait.

2

Pope: A Poet for Posterity

ALEXANDER POPE is the crux on which the first half of this chapter must inevitably focus, but I must touch first on the context, as far as portraiture is concerned, in which one would expect to find him. The English gentleman or aristocrat had been provided with a prototype for his external image by Van Dyck in one magic decade between 1630 and 1640: one can indeed almost suggest that Van Dyck invented the English gentleman, in a statement around which later painters up to Gainsborough, Reynolds, and Sir Thomas Lawrence, and even John Singer Sargent, were to devise endless variations. In terms of style, through the rest of the seventeenth century the English gentleman can be observed in his portraits rising up in a generally dignified but also fluent way. He lives in a world of flowing draperies, cascading curls of wigs, in the grand generalizing and curvaceous amplitude of the baroque. In the general run of work of the two painters who took over successively after Van Dyck as the leading artists of their time, Sir Peter Lely, who died in 1680, and Sir Godfrey Kneller, who carried right on up till his death in 1723, the individuality of their sitters tends to sink from sight. Even so, poets and men of letters too can become indistinguishable from any other men of fashion. Congreve is but one of many examples, painted by Kneller in 1709, in the context of the Kit-cat Club, which was a social and political Whiggish context, but also an intellectual and a literary one. The publisher Tonson was its secretary, and Addison and Steele were members. Congreve as seen as a member of the Club (Kneller painted all of them)[1] has elegance and gesture that are almost foppish, though this is well before Voltaire went to call on him and came away disgusted by Congreve's pretensions to appear as a gentleman of fashion rather than an honest man of letters. This portrait, though, has a vigour and individuality still alive under that wig; in more routine statements Kneller — and his workshop, which became an early prototype of the factory conveyor-belt system — simply accommodated his sitters into a formula.

As illustration consider two Kneller portraits that could be of the

Pl. 42

42 Congreve. By Sir
Godfrey Kneller, 1709

Pls. 43 and 44

same man. They are in fact of different people who sat to Kneller around 1719. One is Addison, the other probably a member of the Sykes family whose identity is long lost, if, indeed, it was ever very clearly recognized. They share a mutual body, dress, and pose, if not quite identical faces. The pose is easy, slightly *de haut en bas*: the paintings are designed to be looked up to, and the gesture has perhaps Olympian overtones, echoes from the Belvedere Apollo. There is no indication that either is a poet, and one doubtless was not.

Yet poets as such could inspire Kneller to some of his finest portraits, and at Cambridge, Trinity happily has two of his masterpieces. Kneller's talent could show itself to be of a very high order and in these does so. The first is one of the greatest figures amongst the great line of Cambridge poets, John Dryden, who came

up to Trinity in 1650 and became in 1668 the first English poet to have the office of Poet Laureate made regally official by warrant. Following his conversion to Catholicism, after the succession of the Catholic James II, in 1685, and his subsequent refusal to recant three years later after the Glorious Protestant Revolution and the arrival of Dutch William, he was deprived of his laurels, but Kneller in a beautiful silvery evocation of Dryden in his old age, in 1697, three years before Dryden's death, shows him reluctant to part anyway with the poet's bays. Kneller, incidentally, was a Catholic too. In his rather earlier portrait of Dryden – about 1693, now in the National Portrait Gallery – the bays were likewise featured as if in stubborn refusal, by that most professional of English poets, to accept the right of anyone to deny them to him. The Trinity portrait belonged to Jacob Tonson, and was surely painted for him.[2]

The other Kneller masterpiece in Trinity came to the College perhaps by a bit of a mistake – given in 1908 by a considerable benefactor to Cambridge, Fairfax Murray, but I suspect under the misapprehension that its subject, Matthew Prior, was a Trinity man, whereas in fact he was a St. John's man. It was painted in 1700 for the Earl of Halifax, one of the first to collect portraits of poets. It is an extraordinary and arresting image, the poet, naked of a wig, rising dark and vertical from subsiding draperies. To see how

43 (*left*) Addison. By Sir Godfrey Kneller, *c.*1719(?)

44 (*right*) 'Mr Sykes'. By Sir Godfrey Kneller

Pl. 45

Pl. 46

45 Dryden. By Sir Godfrey Kneller, 1697

46 Prior. By Sir Godfrey
Kneller, 1700

47 Prior. By A. S. Belle,
1713 or 14

extraordinary, it can be compared with other portraits of Prior, who has quite a rich iconography[3] – to take but one, which shows Prior both in his social and official role, not as poet but as the professional diplomat, civil servant, and man of fashion, and is in the right place (i.e. his own College, St. John's). It was painted in Paris by A. S. Belle, and the engraving of it mentions no poetry, describing its subject with pomp as 'The honourable Matthew Prior Her / late most Sacred Majesty's Plenipotentiary to / Louis the XIV King of France, and one of the / Commissioners of Her Customs'. It is said it was indeed commissioned and paid for by Louis XIV himself. But Prior was also a man of affairs, of business – the first to demonstrate the economic benefits that authors could derive from subscription-based publishing.[4] Poor Dryden was not, writing often in the more traditional mode of the poet, as he said, 'under the spur of poverty', and his complaint is still moving: 'It is enough for one age to have neglected Mr Cowley and starved Mr Butler.'

Pl. 48   A last, perhaps posthumous, look at Dryden, though, shows him tricked out in poetic atmospherics. It was painted by one Maubert, almost miniature in scale, for an unknown purpose, though later it belonged to Horace Walpole at Strawberry Hill, and is now in the National Portrait Gallery. In studied composure he sits his elaborate stool: the drapes drawn back reveal apparently a window with an eagle on its ledge poised for flight to Helicon and Parnassus and the dawn. The eagle bears in its beak a Horatian tag for delivery. At the poet's elbow are ranged the works of his spiritual ancestors. The books are inscribed. One is perhaps unexpected, though surely empirically right: Montaigne. The others are Homer, Virgil, and Horace – but the one open is of course the prime English authority, presider, and local household deity: Shakespeare. Dryden in fact owned a painting of Shakespeare, copied from the Chandos portrait of Shakespeare (see p. 55 and Pl. 59) and specially painted for him by Kneller about 1689. Already by 1668 Dryden had named Shakespeare as the 'Homer of our British poets'. In his long poem to Kneller, thanking the painter for the gift of the portrait, published in the *Miscellanies* of 1694, Dryden has these lines:

> Shakespeare (Thy gift) I place before my sight,
> With awe I ask his blessing ere I write,
> With reverence look on his majestick face,
> Proud to be less, but of, his godlike race . . .

Here bardolatry is clearly under way, at least in the poets' ranks. Bardolatry is a cult necessarily accompanied by votive images.

All through the seventeenth century, as noted earlier, those who wished to know what Shakespeare looked like would have little choice but to consult the image first published in the First Folio of

48 Dryden. By J. Maubert

1623, the engraving by Droeshout, still being repeated in the Fourth
Folio of 1685. But it was not long after that that the poet Nicholas
Rowe decided that a new version of the plays was necessary, and this
duly appeared, edited by Rowe, in 1709. Rowe was also the first to
treat Shakespeare's biography as of intrinsic interest for the works,
and prefaced his edition of the plays with a biographical account that
included some local tradition from Stratford, reported to him by
Betterton. But for the presiding image, in his frontispiece, he used an
engraving based not on the Droeshout engraving nor the Stratford
monument but on the Chandos painting. Modest enough – too
modest, a bit stiff, in that swirling baroque setting with trumpeting
fame winged aloft, and the doting Muses as supporters. All that
business may divert our attention from the portrait to its setting, the
allegorical framework, and it announces, indeed, a curious counterpoint which runs right through the English eighteenth-century
interpretation of Shakespeare's image. In some insular critical
appreciation of the work in the same period, even up to Johnson and

Pl. 49

49 (*above left*) Shakespeare.
By M. van der Gucht, from
Rowe's edition of the Plays,
1709

50 (*above right*) Corneille.
From the 1660 Rouen
edition of his Works

51 (*right*) Shakespeare. By
L. du Guernier, from
Rowe's second edition of
the Plays, 1714

51

51

Mr W.m Shakespeare

52 (*left*) Shakespeare. By G.
Duchange after a drawing
by B. Arlaud, *c*.1709

53 (*below left*) Shakespeare.
By George Vertue, 1719

54 (*below right*) Shakespeare.
By J. Houbraken, 1747

beyond, there appears a faintly defensive strain, as critics, aware of Aristotelian canons of form, had to agree that Shakespeare did not abide by the rules as did the great French tragedians. Naturally — and rightly — they claimed that his superlative virtues made any weakness in that one respect negligible, but it is odd that in his portraiture a French accent is often very clearly discernible: in the case of Rowe's first frontispiece, even blatantly so, for the design is lifted straight from the 1660 Rouen edition of the most severely classical of all French tragedians, Corneille. It is identical, apart from the bust of Corneille himself yielding to Shakespeare's head and shoulders. In fact, the rather dour version of the Chandos transplanted here was evidently not thought to be quite right, not quite in key, and it was replaced five years later, in the second issue of Rowe's edition, in 1714. The 1709 engraving was by an immigrant Dutchman, M. van der Gucht; the 1714 one, considerably freer throughout, is by the Frenchman, L. du Guernier, and the image of Shakespeare that it includes is based on an engraving by yet another Frenchman, G. Duchange, after a drawing based on the Chandos painted by yet another Frenchman or Swiss, called B. Arlaud. Impressions of Duchange's engraving, which is not dated, occur even in some copies of the 1709 edition.[5] This interpretation may seem to modulate our doughty British poet into an almost rococo minor French court poet, but it was to be very widely broadcast, becoming in fact the house mark (and probably shop sign) of the Tonson publishing dynasty in their premises from 1710 in the Strand at the Shakespeare Head, and presiding over best-sellers to be found throughout the literate houses of the land, as on the title-pages of the *Spectator*. Very soon portraits of Shakespeare emerged from the confines of the frontispiece in the printed book, and larger, folio-sized engravings were published, suitable for framing and hanging on the wall. The Chandos portrait remains the source, but the features that emerge from its chrysalis can be very different in characterization, as the two most widely known variants make clear: that engraved by George Vertue in 1719, and that by Houbraken, which appeared in Birch's *Heads* in 1747.

Pl. 53
Pl. 54

By then the proliferation was great, and in other media too — most notably in sculpture, and in sculpture in the context of collections of busts of authors used for the decoration of libraries.[6] This practice had become fashionable by the 1730s, though it started much earlier, and the most spectacular surviving example is that of Trinity College Library, Cambridge. There Wren's intention had originally been to have life-scale statues of classical authors, but this was modified to plaster busts, subsequently supplemented by the remarkable collection of eighteenth- and nineteenth-century marbles on plinths at floor level. Shakespeare, though, is not among them, but he appears elsewhere from the 1730s onwards,

sometimes in a close quartet of superior poetic deities: Shakespeare, Milton, Dryden, and – already – Pope; sometimes in more general assembly, as in the Temple of British Worthies, of about 1732, at Stowe.

The almost abrupt popularization of sculpted portraits at this time, as they move out of the setting of churches and memorial tombs to which they had earlier been almost exclusively confined, is a facet of the classicizing taste of Lord Burlington and the Palladian group. Marble busts go well in marble halls, and furthermore they are rich in heroic echoes of classical antiquity. As such, when of British poets, they become part of that long argument over the relative stature of Ancient and Modern writers that obsessed European critics and historians, and visibly they set moderns in at least parity with classical forebears. If a credible modernity of dress is observed by the retention of the honest British doublet, the conventional drapery about the shoulders adds a hint of toga. The fundamental distinction of character, however, between sculpted busts and painted portraits is of course the lack of colour in the former: in them the pulse and flush of life is stilled, and the image is drained of the accidental ephemera of mortality. They can become, as it were, Platonic

55 The Library, Trinity College, Cambridge. Before the recent cleaning, and the rearrangement of the portrait busts. Byron's statue is at the far end, Tennyson's bust (now moved elsewhere) nearest the spectator on the right

56 Shakespeare. By P. Scheemakers, c.1742(?)

57 Shakespeare. By M. Rysbrack

essences, or lucid and lucent material incorporations of intellect and imagination. If architecture be held to be 'gefrorene Musik', these pale and serene images sometimes evoke 'gefrorener Geist'. When painted black or gilt, as they sometimes were, the impression of icons is even stronger. The fact that they are poets is usually not spelled out by attributes — laurels, bays, pens — but it was normally clear from the context in which they were sited. Pls. 56, 57 and 58

But in whatsoever form, images of the great poets were becoming desiderata for domestic consumption, and, for the practitioners of poetry, perhaps part of the necessary equipment. We have seen Dryden setting up Shakespeare as inspirational image. The artistic quality of the icon from which he asked blessing was not important. As one can see from the actual object that belonged to the late Earl Pl. 58 Fitzwilliam, the copy of the Chandos portrait that Kneller gave him was fairly drear. I doubt if Kneller himself touched it, but assume that it was painted by one of his assistants: it has anyway generalized away almost all the individuality that the Chandos painting had into an anonymous Augustan mask. It is not known in what form Pope first had portraits for similar use, but he had them early on, for already in 1711 he was writing: 'I keep the pictures of Dryden, Milton, Shakespeare, etc., in my chamber, round about me, that the constant remembrance of 'em may keep me always humble.' (In that, they may have failed rather — humility was not to prove one of

58 Shakespeare. By L. F. Roubiliac *c*.1755–60(?)

59 Shakespeare. Painting (from the 'Chandos' portrait) by Sir Godfrey Kneller, *c.*1694

Alexander Pope's most striking qualities, but the sentiment is admirable.) In the same year, 1711, Pope's poem, *The Temple of Fame*, appeared. It echoes, and in part closely, Chaucer's poem, just as Chaucer's is the work amongst his output that most nearly echoes Dante, Virgil, and Ovid. Chaucer has poets – Homer, Virgil, Ovid – high amongst the famous, on pillars: for Pope, poets are predominant, on 'six columns o'er the rest aspiring', and it is to his own installation, not just in that imaginary temple, but in proxy person enduring through libraries and galleries of posterity that I must now attend.

Napoleon, at his coronation, took the imperial crown from the nerveless hands of the officiating Pope, and crowned himself. Alexander Pope's practice was not all that different in principle *vis-à-vis* his own portraits. He did not (as far as we know) paint any self-portraits, but he imposed, or tried to impose, close personal control on their production. Anyone may come to realize that there are quite a lot of portraits of Pope; Voltaire observed, as early as about 1730, that whereas he had noted the portrait of the prime minister hanging over his own chimney-piece, 'I have seen that of Mr Pope in twenty noblemen's houses'. But it is only when one starts to investigate more closely, or browse in W. K. Wimsatt's remarkable book[7] on Pope's portraits, that the full extent is borne in on one. Wimsatt established some sixty-six primary types, or – roughly – original portraits of

Pope. This is a phenomenal number, matched only at this period by royalty, and many of these originals were copied, and then reduplicated and widely disseminated in engravings. The motives behind their proliferation were no doubt mixed, and were also surely given edge by Pope's close personal involvement with the visual arts and with artists. At one stage, with some help from the portrait painter Charles Jervas, he painted on his own, though probably merely copying. This interest, and awareness of quality, may account for the fact that while his period is generally held to be that of the nadir of the English school of painting, in terms of quality several of the portraits of him are well above the average run of the day. A dominant impulse to have oneself portrayed is a normal human vanity, all the more urgent before photography made portraiture cheap, instantaneous, and ubiquitous. In Pope's case vanity was intensified by the need to rectify the tragic twisted reality of his crippled body with an image worthy of the lucid, beautifully articulated construction and spirit of his poetry — the need, very literally, to put the image straight. When the sum of his portraits is surveyed, it reads like a willed, highly controlled, projection by Pope of his person into posterity.

60 Pope. By an unknown artist, 1695

The story begins very early, with a portrait of Pope as a boy aged seven.[8] This was noted early on by Joseph Spence and, like the comparable portrait of Milton as a child, was evidently commissioned by doting parents. Showing a perfectly normal child, bright as a button, it has pathos, for his crippling handicap had not yet afflicted him. But it is also witness of Pope's loving care of his image, even retrospectively, for the sprig of laurel or bay in his hand was not originally included in precocious prophecy by his parents, but was, according to Spence, painted in by Charles Jervas later in Pope's lifetime. The painter is unknown, and the portrait is in the Osborn collection in the Beineke Library at Yale.   Pl. 60

The image is of about 1695, and thereafter Pope's appearance is uncharted for perhaps twenty years. Although his physical affliction set in only some two years after the painting of his likeness as a child — according to Spence, 'the perpetual application he fell into . . . changed his form, and ruin'd his constitution' — by the time he was in his mid-twenties he had learned to live with it, and indeed in his portraits to discount it. So in the first image of his precocious maturity, finished probably late in 1714 by his friend   Pl. 61
Charles Jervas, his appearance suggests a fastidious elegance — of

61 Pope. By C. Jervas, 1714

body no less than of dress and mood.[9] His person appears delicate, certainly. As painting, it is evidence too, already, of Pope's ability — not always, but quite often — to inspire his portrayers to do better than they normally knew how. The composition, pose, and so on are entirely conventional, yet the sensibility of the sitter — in the features as in the admirably expressive hand — is indicated in a subtlety of drawing to which Jervas did not usually aspire. It even, for all its delicacy, and a clear indication that the sitter is not of a large physique, avoids any implication of the hunched back, while no one, I think, would infer from this image that its original was only 4 feet 6 inches high. He was, I suspect, a little more than that, but it was as four feet six that Sir Joshua Reynolds, who glimpsed Pope in person at Lord Oxford's sale in 1742, is said to have remembered him.[10] At that sale there was at least one portrait of Pope included, but not this one, though in fact it belonged to Harley, Earl of Oxford. It belonged originally to Prior, was bought by Harley after Prior's death in 1721, and was given by him to another Oxford, the University, and now hangs in the Bodleian Library. Pope clearly approved of it, as Vertue's engraving from it appeared in the first collected edition of the *Works*, 1717, though it may have been sparked off in the first place in the build-up to the publication of the translation of Homer's *Iliad* in 1715.

Pl. 62

Jervas's other portrait[11] of Pope, though not dated, seems to show the poet at much the same period, and does have very specific reference to Homer. It is also much more ambitious in composition: Pope sits in the traditional attitude of poetic melancholy, head on hand, eyes fixed dreamily on some vision beyond. The lady behind — usually interpreted as a portrait of Martha Blount, though if so perhaps Martha Blount also somewhat in character as the Muse — is reaching a book down from the shelves. The design, that counterpoint of poses of man and woman, seems to be the first of several variants on the theme, the most famous being that by Hogarth of Garrick and Mrs Garrick in the Royal Collection. The bust on the pedestal on the left is Homer and is closely related to the blind Hellenistic type, specifically to the version in the Farnese Collection (the type illustrated from the British Museum version in Pl. 2), which was engraved, from a drawing of it by Jervas, for Volume I of Pope's *Homer*. Pope's own marble bust of Homer, in his library, may have been of the same type. It is, incidentally, the first appearance of Homer, as presider, in a portrait of an English poet. It is also, I think — apart from Van Dyck's Sir John Suckling — the first life-scale whole-length painting of an English poet seen as a poet. Although this is a carefully contrived, indeed somewhat pretentious, composition, Pope's person seems less self-assured, less comfortable in elegance, than in Jervas's other portrait. He seems a little

62 Pope. By C. Jervas, *c.*1715—20(?)

63 (*above left*) Pope. By Sir
Godfrey Kneller, 1716

64 (*above right*) Pope. By Sir
Godfrey Kneller, 1721

65 (*right*) Pope. Medal, by J.
Dassier, 1741 (enlarged)

awkwardly disposed, not relaxed, about shoulders and thighs, in
his chair, and either the chair is unusually large or its inhabitant
rather small. Two versions are known, one, from the National
Portrait Gallery, now on loan to Marble Hill at Twickenham, and
another in a private collection, but of neither is the original owner
known.

The Jervas portraits are followed by a sequence of no fewer than
three by Sir Godfrey Kneller, between 1716 and 1722. Of the first[12]
of these some dozen versions are known, witness to some pressure of
demand, though some of the copies may not be contemporary. It
was engraved by John Smith in mezzotint in 1717 — a good large
engraving, like Vertue's before it, and suitable for framing; it was
copied in due course for inclusion amongst portrait sets of poets and
worthies. It shows Pope informally, wearing the strange turban-like
velvet hat that the English gentry wore in their leisure moments, to
protect the shaven or close-cropped heads from draughts when they
took their wigs off. He appears to be standing, in a landscape, with a
folio of Homer open at the opening lines of *Iliad* IX — and Homer in
the Greek, not in Pope's English. It is reminiscent of Van Dyck's
Suckling, both in setting and in the very close echo of the pose,
though the habit of reading large folios out of doors still seems rather
uncomfortable, especially standing up. A repetition of this portrait,
signed and dated by Kneller, 1719, now at Raby Castle, is probably
the other portrait of Pope that belonged to Harley, Earl of Oxford.
In correspondence with Harley, Pope refers to this portrait apparently alongside one of the poet Cleveland, which reminds one
that Harley collected for his library at Wimpole a remarkable array
of poets' portraits. It is, however, also to be noted that Harley's
collection included a very early example of demand precipitating a
rather doubtful supply in this field. Harley's portrait called Cleveland
is now in the Tate Gallery, where it is shown as a fine example of the
work of its painter, Isaac Fuller. That it truly is, but cleaning has
revealed that the subject of the painting was originally some
architect, who had been overpainted to transform him into the poet
Cleveland before Oxford bought it.[13]

In Kneller's second painting[14] of Pope, the classical reference is not
spelled out but is intrinsically even stronger. It was originated in
1721; is again known in several versions, though not as many as in
the case of the 1716 type; and, again, was engraved in mezzotint
some time later by J. Faber the younger, in 1738. It is consciously an
exercise on a medallic theme. Profile portraits were rare in painting,
but normal in medals. Pope had responded to Addison's three
Dialogues on Medals with a complimentary poem to Addison on
them, with a plea to British artists to celebrate her heroes in medallic
form, 'emulous of Greek and Roman fame'.

Pls. 63, 64, and 67

> Then future ages with delight shall see
> How Plato's, Bacon's, Newton's looks agree;
> Or in fair series laurell'd Bards be shown,
> A Virgil there, and here an Addison . . .

In fact it was the Renaissance rather than antiquity that liked to celebrate its poets in medallic form; medals of Italian poets from Dante through Petrarch to Ariosto are both fairly frequent and admirably expressive. The double-side form enables the artist to present the likeness on one side and an emblem on the other side, as for example Poggini's of Ariosto showing a hand with shears cutting a serpent's tongue out. It was not a medium that the English adopted for the celebration of their native authors, for all that they earlier on had been assiduous collectors of classical coins and of medals; Pope was about the first, or amongst a group of the first, English poets to be so celebrated. The medal comes much later in Pope's career, but may be best considered in the context of Kneller's profile painting. It was made by a Swiss medallist, Jacques Dassier, in 1741. Dassier's father had had a project for a set including Chaucer, Spenser, Shakespeare, Milton by 1733, but that seems never to have materialized and did not include Pope. The son's medal of Pope does not attempt any illustration on the back, where the words *Poeta*
Pl. 65   *Anglus*, with date, were thought adequate.[15]

In fact, Kneller's profile is richer in allusion, having not only the classic profile, toga'd, laureate, but the image set within that antique symbol of eternity, the *uroboros*, the serpent biting its own tail. Also 'laureate' is not literally correct for the foliage girding the poet's brow; it is clearly ivy. Especially recondite theorists distinguished between the significance of ivy and that of bays or laurel. Pope himself, in the *Essay on Criticism*, has 'The Poet's Bays and Critick's
Pl. 64   Ivy', but was the first to allocate ivy to critics; a little later, Kneller's profile may not have seemed so becoming to him, as in the *Dunciad* ivy is called 'creeping, dirty, dangling, courtly' — and, in general, a contemptible attribute of the Poet Laureate. By then Pope himself, abetted by his friend the portrait painter Richardson, was settling for bays for his own image.

Kneller's third and last Pope, 1722, was painted for Lord Harcourt's library and has descended direct in the Harcourt
Pl. 67   family.[16] The mood is as in the Jervas whole-length — pensive poetic melancholy, head on hand. There is, however, no bust of Homer — instead Pope's elbow rests on a folio clearly inscribed with Homer's name, and this time in English and Greek. No landscape here, but rather, intensified by the loose dress, a hint of midnight oil in the poet's study. Though amongst Kneller's last works, which are usually thought to contain his weakest, this is a superb portrait. It also was engraved in large quarto mezzotint by G. White, and during the

nineteenth century became especially admired, partly for reasons that comparison with one of Joseph Severn's portraits of Keats may hint at. There is a pallor, a hint of ill health, and aloneness which make of this a romantic portrait before its time. In its own time, however, it was taken advantage of by the enemies that the *Dunciad* so crisply provoked, and the best-known 'antipapal' caricature is based horribly upon it, published in 1729, and then again in slightly altered form the same year as frontispiece to the anonymous assault called *Pope Alexander's Supremacy and Infallibility examined . . .*[17] In this shape the image obviously enjoyed some circulation, and it can be found, *inter alia*, pinned to the wall in Hogarth's painting of the *Distress'd Poet*, 1735. Its significance, in context with the distressed poet's hopeless conflict with poverty and domesticity in his garret, is not quite certain, but doubtless it is not intended as complimentary to Pope.[18] Pope, for Hogarth, was too closely identified with Lord Burlington's set, especially the painter and designer William Kent, who was Hogarth's foe.

Pl. 130

Pl. 66

Pope himself anyway was not, and had no intention of finding himself, in comparable deprivation to that of the distressed poet, which image might perhaps have served for Dryden, though in greater *extremis* than even he was ever pushed to. Economic independence was at last a possibility — though it has never become a certainty — for members of the literary profession. Prior's exploitation of the subscription system of publishing had indicated one aid to independence, and the 1709 Copyright Act opened up another.[19] An author's work was established as his property, to be used as bargaining basis for contracts with publishers and booksellers. The measures did not protect Pope entirely from pirate publishers, but they certainly helped him to a position from which, by 1723, he could write: 'I take myself to be the only scribbler of my time, of any degree of distinction, who never received any Places from the Establishment, any Pension from the Court, or any Presents from a Ministry. I desire to preserve this Honour untainted to my Grave.'[20] His was not the great Declaration of Independence itself, which was to come in Samuel Johnson's immortal rebuke to Lord Chesterfield. It comes close to it, but Pope had a useful network, if not so much of actual patronage from the aristocracy, then of alliance across the country, and part of the maintenance system of this network was the presence of Pope's image in their houses.

If, however, a considerable number of paintings of him, originals and replicas, were to be found, as Voltaire noted, in the houses of the great, the distribution in real quantity was via engravings: four out of the five paintings we have mentioned so far were engraved. Mezzotint engraving, one branch of art in which the British have never been surpassed, was coming into its prime, offering convincing

66 Pope. Anonymous,
'Martini Scribleri', *c.*1729

Pl. 69

equivalents of richness of texture, of light and shade, if not of colour, to those qualities in the original painting. Control of the original was exercised in Pope's case by the choice of the best painters available, and, as we have noted, managing to extract the best out of them that their talents could rise to, no doubt with some degree of criticism and encouragement. First there was Charles Jervas, and then, until his death in 1723, Sir Godfrey Kneller. With Kneller's rival, Michael Dahl, Pope did not succeed so well, emerging in a very routine variation on the old cliché for men of letters, as in Raphael's portrait of Tommaso Inghirami, pen in hand, eyes gaping upwards for inspiration – though that too, of 1726, exists in several versions, and was likewise mezzotinted.[21] The real successor to Kneller, as far as Pope was concerned, was the painter Jonathan Richardson. As painter, Richardson was normally of a rather boring, honest competence. He was, though, also originator of a very remarkable collection of Old Master drawings, and, more importantly in our context, a writer himself on matters relating both to the visual arts and to poetry, and a devotee of English poets living and dead. Amongst the dead, he revered Milton especially; as is clear from his voluminous book on Milton's work, this devotion was scarcely this side of idolatry, and is summarized in undoubtedly earnest if rather odd form in a painting by Richardson that is almost a very belated

67 Pope. By Sir Godfrey Kneller, 1722

68 Pope. By Jonathan
Richardson, with the dog
'Bounce', *c*.1718

69 Pope. By Michael Dahl,
1726

70 By Jonathan Richardson; Richardson and his son with an apparition of Milton

and secular restatement of the donor portrait. In this, instead of supplicants before the Virgin and Child, there appear Jonathan Richardson and his son, in respectful if somewhat proprietary alignment with the conjured-up vision of Milton.[22] Richardson's cultivation of poetry and poets certainly is in the antique tradition of interdependence between poetry and painting – *Ut pictura poesis*. The painting of himself with Milton is perhaps not to be seen as representing mere acolytes in the presence of deity, but as a claim on behalf equally of painters and poets for parity in fame and immortality. In his writing on art, Richardson indeed suggests with some firmness that the painter of genius ranks higher than the poet of genius, the argument being that poets and painters have to have very closely comparable talents, but that the painter has also to be a 'Curious Artificer', which the poet does not. This reverses the old contention, that painters were not to be considered true practitioners of the liberal arts, or even gentlemen, because, being manual workers, they were merely craftsmen. On the contrary, said Richardson, Raphael, having that extra talent, 'is not only Equal, but Superior to a Virgil, or a Livy, a Thucydides, or a Homer'.[23] In real life, though, Richardson was far from averse to poets: first, his especial affections were settled on Prior, and after his death, almost remorselessly on Pope. There are over eighty portraits of Pope

Pl. 70

Alex. Pope.

71 Pope. By Jonathan
Richardson

associated with Richardson; a number of these are later copies, but
about a dozen of the originals are etchings, of which many
impressions of course exist. On the other hand, over thirty are
drawings: Richardson was accused of narcissism in his own time, of
drawing his own self-portrait once a day, but Pope was obviously a
subject for constant practice. They were close acquaintances,
perhaps, rather than friends, from Pope's viewpoint anyway, and
saw each other quite frequently. Many of Richardson's drawings are
clearly from the life, others seem exercises in the search for the perfect
image.

Richardson's opening is a full-scale painting of Pope in a
combination of the poetic melancholic head-on-hands convention
with the reading-of-a-folio-in-landscape one.[24] One version of this,
painted for Pope's friend Lord Cobham at Hagley (and still there),
Pl. 68   adds in Pope's great dog, Bounce. That was about 1718, but the
subsequent association, lasting until Pope's death in 1744, produced
portraits concentrating on the poet's head. The drawings might be
slight and intimate – there's even a Pope asleep – but can read as
practices for an ideal image. There are classic profiles especially, as in
the etching used for the *Letters* of 1737, but also full face, three-
Pl. 71   quarter face, and some of the drawings show crowns of bay leaves.
There were also strange variations, attempts as it were to accom-

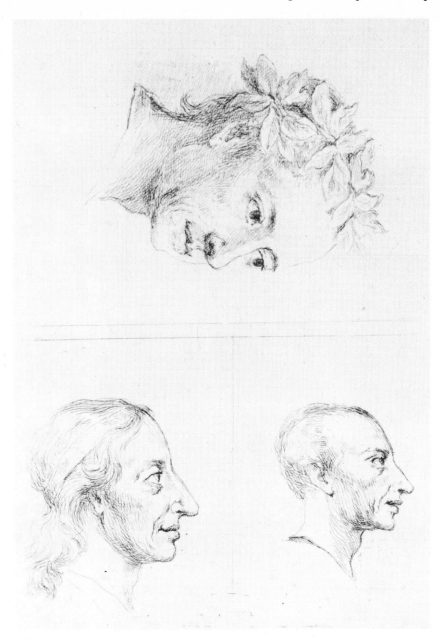

72 Pope. 'Milton into Pope', by Jonathan Richardson, *c.*1734−5(?)

modate earlier poets from the British poets' Parnassus within Pope's image; even to conflate an ideal poet, with Pope's image dominant: Pope as Chaucer, and then, in a strange multiple image that Richardson actually etched, Pope as Milton. There are far too many Richardsons[25] to illustrate here, and towards the end they decline, though not unmovingly so. The last, dated 1742, perhaps reflects something both of the poet's shrunken infirmity in his last years, and Richardson's uncertainty of hand following a stroke.[26] It contrasts

Pl. 72

Poeta Anglus,
OB: Aº 1744 ÆTAT: 57

73 Pope. By J. Faber, after
J. B. van Loo, 1742

with the last painting of Pope in the kind of tradition in which
Richardson had first painted him — a half-length seated in the poetic
melancholic head-on-hand pose with eyes heavenward, painted by
the French society painter, Van Loo.[27] Van Loo enjoyed considerable success in London between 1738 and 1742, and this is said
to be of 1742, the same year as Richardson's last portrait. Van Loo's
success lay partly in his highly skilled blend of naturalism with
French chic. He was celebrated for his ability to capture a likeness: as
Vertue noted, 'his great success in likeness, naturally without
flattery — or raising the character'. Here the character, though, is
certainly, if not 'raised', shown posed to betray no physical infirmity
or weariness of age. One version was painted for Murray, later first
Earl of Mansfield, and another for Lord Gowra, later Earl of Upper
Ossory, and this type of portrait was to become perhaps the best
Pl. 73   known of all, widely disseminated by copies and derivative

74 Pope. By William Hoare

engravings. But it is time to check the degree of 'raising' of character in Pope's authorized portraiture by a couple of unauthorized glimpses.

The first is very well known, by William Hoare, who had a well-established practice at the fashionable spa of Bath.[28] He painted one formal portrait of Pope, of which Hoare's son, Prince Hoare, later recalled that, when sitting for it, Pope showed an anxiety to conceal the deformity of his person, and had a cloak thrown over his shoulders, and that while 'Mr Hoare was painting that part of the picture He came behind Him and said "He need not be very particular about the shoulders"'. The image of Pope by Hoare that is best remembered, though, was unauthorized, and was 'particular about the shoulders': it was drawn in the library of Ralph Allen's house, Prior Park, near Bath, while Pope was talking to Allen and others, including Warburton. It was first published in Warton's edition of Pope's *Works* in 1797, with a note that it was done without

Pl. 74

75 (*left*) Pope. By Lady Burlington (? or William Kent)

76 (*right*) Pope in his Grotto. By Lady Burlington (? or William Kent)

Pope's knowledge ('Pope would never have forgiven the Painter had he known it'). Its publication aroused some censure, but I think it was neither published nor originally drawn in malice but as an exclamation in wonder, even affection perhaps, at the paradox it represented. Surely so was the other unauthorized glimpse jotted down by Lady Burlington (or perhaps William Kent), catching Pope unawares about a favourite diversion, a game of cards.[29]

The self-awareness, the vanity, that wished to exclude that view was far more than merely defensive, or pathetic. Pope's vanity was magisterially intense, yet swelled, and not least in his actual portraits, the scope of his own image to embrace the poetic vocation itself, its classic dignity and its independence. In no medium was this more successfully achieved than in sculpture. Here Pope was fortunate in his interpreters. Two of the three most impressive sculptors who flourished in England in his lifetime were of considerable calibre. All three were immigrants, Scheemakers, Rysbrack, and Roubiliac. Pope was carved by both Rysbrack and Roubiliac, the last of these a very remarkable virtuoso. Rysbrack's first marble, now in the

Pl. 77

Athenaeum, was the earliest, 1730.[30] Though apparently not approved – and indeed as physical likeness difficult to reconcile with the sum of evidence constituted by other portraits of Pope – it is truly a heroic image in its cool and serene gravity. Sustaining that sometimes difficult balance between baroque movement and classic restraint which the English Palladians essayed, it achieves almost a pre-Romantic or a neo-Hellenistic glamour. But the definitive three-dimensional image was to be achieved a little later by the French sculptor, Roubiliac, in a series of busts between 1738 and

Pls. 78 and 79

1741.[31] Roubiliac could at times be positively rococo in style, but these are both more severely classical, in their restraint and simplicity as in their use of antique drapery, and more definitively and subtly

individualized than Rysbrack's. Roubiliac is said to have observed
that Pope's face indicated 'much affliction with headache', 'from the
contracted appearance of the skin above the eyebrows'.[32] An
extraordinary face, remembered Joshua Reynolds, not an everyday
countenance: a pallid studious look; not merely a sharp keen
countenance, but something grand, like Cicero's.[33] Here the
analogy with classical antiquity becomes explicit, as nowhere else in
his lifetime perhaps except in one painting. That, a laureate profile, in
the National Portrait Gallery, is attributed to Richardson, but is so
much more lively, more bold, more simply grand than in any other
painting known to me by Richardson that I almost doubt it to be his
unless it is another example of Pope's inspiring his portraitists beyond
their average abilities.[34] This strong and broadly painted image is a
heroic one, yet sensitive to accommodate the rest of Reynolds's
memory, after his observation of the smallness, the deformity, the
little sword — 'he had a large and very fine eye, and a long handsome
nose; his mouth had those peculiar marks which are always found in
the mouths of crooked persons; and the muscles which ran across his
cheeks were so strongly marked as to appear like small cords . . .' It
would be nice if this portrait could be attributed to Reynolds. It is
not impossible that it is posthumous, and inspired by Kneller's
classicizing profile painted in 1721.

Pl. 80

77 Pope. By Michael
Rysbrack, 1730

78 Pope. By L. F. Roubiliac, 1741

79 Pope. Variations on a theme, by L. F. Roubiliac

80 (*facing*) Pope. Attributed to Jonathan Richardson

There I must leave Pope and his portraits. Their relevance to his poetry may leave some unroused, and is anyway not be resolved in words, but when a great gathering of them was assembled at the National Portrait Gallery in 1961, it was obvious that one text, and one only, was acceptable to preside over the exhibition; the most famous I suppose of all passages from his work: the eighteen lines from the opening of Epistle Two of the *Essay on Man* that begin: 'Know then Thyself, presume not God to scan, / The proper study of mankind is man . . .'

One type of portrait that might seem to be denied Pope was the full life-scale whole-length celebration in form of the heroic standing statue. As far as life-scale statues are concerned, Pope still awaits his apotheosis, though on a smaller scale, as we shall see in a moment, a reconciliation of his figure with a representation of the whole body was felt to be acceptable. Meanwhile, his incorporation in the shrines in the Temples of Fame in various forms of leading English poets proceeded. Roubiliac produced perhaps half a dozen variations in marble of his bust of Pope, and also plaster casts from moulds. Sets of poets' busts were becoming almost a commonplace in gentlemen's libraries,[35] and could be bought from statuaries like the Cheeres' workshops at Hyde Park Corner. Pope himself had a set of four marbles by Scheemakers that were commissioned and given to him by Frederick, Prince of Wales in 1735 (Spenser, Shakespeare, Milton, Dryden); these are less than half-size (as were many later plaster sets), more perhaps decorative bibelots than heroic icons, but they are among the earliest I know. There was a rather strange delay in the peopling of English libraries with busts in fact, for Wren's example at Trinity was established by the 1690s, and relevant literary authority was not lacking. Many libraries would have had, for example, Evelyn's translation of Gabriel Naudé's *Instructions Concerning Creating of a Library*, published in 1661, with a whole chapter on the 'Ornament and Decoration necessary to be Observed'. It was Evelyn likewise who recorded that he ever looked upon a library 'with the Reverence of a Temple'. By 1749, Lord Chesterfield had equipped his own library[36] – which he claimed with no false modesty to be the best room in Europe – in his new house in Mayfair with a range of paintings of poets. The centre-piece was the Shakespeare (discussed above, Pl. 41), and the range went up to and included Pope, while Pope again was the fourth in a quartet of busts that Chesterfield shipped over to his friend Mme de Bocage in Paris in 1751, the others being Shakespeare, Milton, and Dryden.

The ceremonial setting-up of busts in a real shrine, in fact a National Pantheon of poets, had by then been going on for fifty years.[37] The germ of this was established by Nicholas Bingham in

1555, when he erected the monument to Chaucer in the north
transept of Westminster Abbey: this was retrospective, by a century
and a half, and was painted but had no bust. In 1599, Spenser was
buried close by, and for him Anne Clifford, great patroness, set up a
memorial, though again without portrait, in 1620; she then, after
1631, did the same for Drayton, and his was the first to be provided
with a laureate portrait bust. The real peopling of Poets' Corner with
images did not, however, come until the two decades within 1720
and 1740. Then there were added busts for Ben Jonson, Samuel
Butler, Milton, Dryden, and so up to Gay, Rowe, and Prior. After
Pope's death in 1744, he was not added – he was a Catholic, and is
buried at Twickenham – and he remains the major lack, of any
memorial at all, in that strange shrine. By the time of his death, the
then greatest gap had been filled. Agitation for a memorial to

81 Shakespeare. By Peter
Scheemakers, erected 1741

Shakespeare in the Abbey goes back to at least 1726, but only in 1741 was it finally unveiled.[38] Pope was on the committee that presided over its gestation – a very Palladian group, headed by Lord Burlington in person, and including his chosen architect and designer, William Kent. Kent designed the monument, and it was carved by the least of the three best sculptors working at the time in England, Scheemakers. It is a competent piece, though one may regret it is not rather more than competent; it conveys a somewhat uncomfortably crouched feeling, as though the marble block had proved too small to accommodate the original conception. That, though, may be Kent's failure rather than the sculptor's, and the 'programme' of the project no doubt is the committee's, including those busts on the pedestal – who are Elizabeth I, Henry V, and Richard III, and why *them*, as Walpole not unreasonably asked, and why, rather lacking in architectural decorum, *there*? The mood is, inevitably in such a setting, elegiac; the traditional poetic melancholic head-on-hand, pointing to the famous lines (in slightly garbled form) from *The Tempest* – the *Cloudcupt* [sic] *Towers, the Gorgeous Palaces* . . . Formally, almost equally inevitably, the statue derives from classical precedents: the melancholic cross-legged standing figure recurs in English portraits from Hilliard's masterpiece of the young man in roses onwards, while a direct classical inspiration may have come from famous antique statues like the Leaning Faun, or Hercules with his club. This is the Palladian Shakespeare; Johnson was to note some twenty years later that 'Shakespeare may now begin to assume the dignity of an ancient', but Shakespeare, in his busts and statues, had by then already done so. His costume here, though, is not classical, yet neither is it historically accurate as Elizabethan. It is that strange garb, almost fancy dress, that the eighteenth century derived from Van Dyck.[39] Portrait painters, up to Reynolds and Gainsborough, loved to dress their sitters in it: not only was it more fluent and picturesque than Georgian costume but it surely had glamorous overtones carried on from that brilliant and doomed Caroline court, so very much more inspiring than the often tedious decorum of Georgian court and society. The head, on the other hand, derives from the Chandos painting, though perhaps via the engraving by du Guernier rather than that by George Vertue.

It was surely fitting that the supreme luminary of the English Parnassus should be represented in the Abbey by a statue rather than, as the rest of them, by a mere bust, and fitting too that this statue has a very early place in the extension of the practice of erecting statues to lesser mortals than kings and queens. The English were now moving to celebrate their heroes of intellect and imagination as well as monarchs and military commanders in full-scale marble, and they

82 Shakespeare. Scheemakers's statue, detail

inspired some splendid images which are nowadays too little considered. Oxford and Cambridge both have masterpieces of this kind. At Oxford, in Christ Church Library, there is Rysbrack's admirable John Locke, of 1757, a convinced and convincing vision of the prophet of the Enlightenment in terms of a prophet of religion, demanding indeed a secular temple for its setting.[40] At Cambridge, there is Roubiliac's rapt and haunting evocation of 1755 of Newton, in Trinity College Chapel. Wordsworth's lines on this are not as often recalled as is his sonnet on King's Chapel, but they deserve to be:

> . . . Newton, with his prism and silent face,
> The marble index of a mind for ever
> Voyaging through strange seas of thought alone.[41]

Scheemakers's Shakespeare is not of that order, yet it is not, and never was, to be ignored. Its unveiling was a huge success; railings had to be erected to keep the crowds off. Full-scale replicas or near-replicas were produced, and it had a continuing progeny.

Pl. 56

Scheemakers's standard bust of Shakespeare relates physiognomically closely to it, and was to prove perhaps the most popular source for subsequent production of library busts.

Before coming to the descendants of the statue, I must glance at an area of this subject to which alone a book could be devoted: the involvement of the greatest actor of the century, David Garrick, with Shakespeare's image.[42] Garrick's first appearance on the London stage, at Goodman's Fields, in March 1741, was in an entertainment, *Harlequin Student*, in which serious drama — personified by a copy actually on stage of the newly unveiled Westminster Abbey statue — rocked the forces of pantomime and burlesque. Garrick's association with Shakespeare's image continued until his retirement in 1776, and even after his death in 1779. His

Pl. 83

monument by Henry Webber, set up in 1797, confronting that of Shakespeare in the Abbey, shows him parting the curtains for the final bow — a theatricality that scandalized Charles Lamb. Above him is a benign medallion profile of Shakespeare, and below, an eloquent epitaph, closing on the couplet that, till the end of time —

> Shakespeare and Garrick like twin-stars shall shine
> And earth irradiate with a beam divine.

In between time, Garrick had appropriated Shakespeare's image almost as his trade mark, or house mark. He was the first of the great actor-managers to understand the job of impresario, not least the importance of publicity and public relations; his relationship with Shakespeare had a strong element of the proprietary in it, and he would no doubt have liked to claim a monopoly on him. Most of this is expressed in Gainsborough's portrait of him, destroyed, alas, in the

Pl. 84

disastrous fire at Stratford Town Hall in 1946.[43] Garrick surely

83 Garrick. Monument, by Henry Webber, erected 1797

indicated how he wished to be painted, Gainsborough equally surely had no objection to painting Garrick, but he had grave reservations about the bust of Shakespeare, being dismayed at the quality of the source material available. He said he meant 'to take the form' from existing portraits 'just enough to preserve his likeness past the doubt of all blockheads at first sight, and supply a *soul* from his works'. I think he was probably working mainly from some version of the Chandos painting, and found it, to say the least, inadequate: 'it is impossible that such a mind and ray of heaven could shine with such a face and pair of eyes as that picture has; so, as I said before, damn that.' Gainsborough's portrait was begun about 1766, but Garrick's celebration of his idol was well under way before then. A decade before, he had had built a small but grandly proportioned private temple for his presiding genius in his garden at Hampton. Into this, in 1758, he put a full-scale marble statue carved for him by Roubiliac.

84 Garrick. By Thomas Gainsborough, 1769 (destroyed 1946)

Zoffany's painting, 1762, of Mr and Mrs Garrick on the steps of the temple, with tea being brought on from the right, is an enchanting specimen of the easy and familiar domesticity into which Georgian society could accommodate its heroics.[44] The flank of the statue is just visible within, and though the temple itself still stands, Garrick left the statue ('for the use of the Publick') to the British Museum, where it presides over the centre of Smirke's great long King's Library. Roubiliac no doubt considered the commission as a challenge to outdo Scheemakers's effort in Westminster Abbey, and surely he succeeded.[45] In one way his task was perhaps easier in that he was not constrained by any funereal monumental context; on the other hand, the programme of the composition — pose, accessories, etc. — was probably no less tightly laid down by Garrick, and the story indeed that Garrick sat or rather stood ('Behold the Bard of Avon!') for the original model is irresistible. The pose represents

Pl. 86

Pl. 85

The inscription on the pedestal reads:

MARBLE STATUE OF WILLIAM SHAKESPEARE
BY L. F. ROUBILIAC SIGNED AND DATED 1758
Formerly in the Temple of Shakespeare
in the garden of Garrick's Villa at Hampton
Bequeathed by David Garrick, 1779

85 Shakespeare. By L. F. Roubiliac, 1757/8

86 Garrick. By Johann
Zoffany, 1762

clearly the poet at work, the mind in action admirably expressed in
the alert reflectiveness of the body and head, with almost 'the poet's
eye in a fine frenzy rolling'. Compared with the pensive sobriety of
the Abbey statue, this has the movement, the ripple of life of the
rococo rather than the baroque, with, once again, a slightly French
accent, an elegant nonchalance as in that slipper so slightly loose on
the foot, plus a reminder that were it not for Houdon, Roubiliac's
stature in the ranks of the great sculptors of the eighteenth century
would be better recognized than it is as yet.

Shakespeare's image appeared elsewhere in Garrick's personal
equipment – on his book-plate, for example, as on his Shakespearian
armchair, carved from the notorious mulberry tree from Stratford
which was producing relics already as inexhaustibly as the true cross.
But the great act of public worship came later: the famous Stratford
Jubilee of 1769, three days long – a slightly belated celebration of
the bicentenary of Shakespeare's birth. Produced and directed by

Garrick, who gave the two paintings — the Gainsborough of himself, a Benjamin Wilson of Shakespeare,[46] both now destroyed — and also a version of the Westminster Abbey statue, still to be seen on the wall of Stratford Town Hall. Even now, with the Jubilee's echoes long stilled and its third day indeed drowned in torrential English rain, the occasion marks the full establishment of Shakespeare in the popular imagination of the nation, as its supreme eminence. In a specially built rotunda, Garrick declaimed his ode in front of the statue — ''Tis he, 'tis he, the God of our idolatry.' Processions, a dinner, speeches, fireworks, a ball. There were Shakespeare favours with medallion portraits. Garrick was painted, yet again, as Steward gazing on a medallic portrait of Shakespeare carved from the mulberry tree. The national press coverage was considerable, though not all entirely respectful, while, perhaps owing to rain, the whole show was financially not a success. Garrick was not all that disturbed, for the full metropolitan impact came when he re-staged the whole thing at Drury Lane. As a theatrical spectacular there, it proved almost the smash hit of the century,

Pl. 84
Pl. 87

Pl. 169

Pl. 88

Pl. 89

87 Shakespeare. By Benjamin Wilson, *c.*1768

Mr Garrick reciting the Ode, in honor of Shakespeare, at the Jubilee at Stratford; with the Musical Performers &c.

88 Garrick. Garrick declaiming his Shakespeare Ode at the Stratford Jubilee, 1769

totalling 153 performances over three seasons. Its success as spectacle, close on pantomime, is somewhat ironic in view of Garrick's tenacious struggle to vindicate the values of true drama in contrast to those of the burlesque. It took Shakespeare's most popular actual play, *Romeo and Juliet*, twenty-five seasons, 1747–76, in Garrick's time, to reach 142 performances. A final glimpse — though there are many others I have not illustrated — of Garrick's and Shakespeare's interdependence. Early on, in 1757, a critic had acclaimed Garrick's rejuvenation of the English stage by establishing 'Nature, Shakespeare and himself'. A perhaps too literal translation of that into Pl. 90   visual images was presented to Garrick by his colleagues on his retirement in 1776; painted in enamel on gold by Cipriani, it shows Garrick toga'd, with dramatic masks, unveiling a term on which are somewhat awkwardly united Shakespeare and Nature. Shakespeare is pointing to his head to indicate his dependence on his partner, inexhaustible Nature, in the shape of the many-bosomed Ephesian Diana.[47]

That, however, is a freak. The staple image which became part of the small change of English culture in three-dimensional form, part, indeed, of its very furniture, proved to be that of Scheemakers's

89 Garrick. By C. Watson, 1784, after R. E. Pine. The Stratford Jubilee re-staged at Drury Lane

90 Garrick. Enamel on gold medallion, by Cipriani, 1776

Abbey statue. The grand, like Lord Pembroke at Wilton, might have full-scale copies; there is the one Garrick gave to Stratford, and another is at Drury Lane. But in miniature it became very popular — at first, in the 1750s and 1760s, modulated in porcelain by Chelsea and Bow into rococo polychrome prettiness (the very earliest, indeed, in the incongruous form of a miniature scent-bottle); then it settled back more staidly into more classical sobriety but often if not always now paired with Milton. Not, as I have indicated, with Pope, although it is in a form inspired by the Westminster Abbey statue of Shakespeare that Pope makes his only appearance, other than in Hoare's drawing and in malign caricature, as a whole-length standing figure.[48] The pose indeed, on a small scale, infected the whole breed of English poets. Cross-legged, leaning on plinths, elegantly draped and with a book or two, from Spenser to Pope, they were available in sets, about 18 inches high, from the Cheere workshop. It is a strange yet somehow compulsive posture, and neither the Romantic poets nor the Victorian ones were to prove able to discard it entirely.

91 (*left*) Shakespeare and Milton. Chelsea/Bow rococo porcelain figures, *c*.1760–70

92 (*below left*) Shakespeare and Milton. Neo-classic variations on the Chelsea/Bow figures

93 (*right*) Pope. Lead statuette, from the workshop of John Cheere, 1749

3

Byron and the Romantic Image

THE most successful, in popular terms, of eighteenth- (or mid-eighteenth-)century developments of portraits of Shakespeare was the Westminster Abbey statue by Scheemakers. Essentially a classicizing figure, it was not one likely to consort very happily with the prototypical image of the Romantic Poet. Or so one would think, even allowing for the fact that it is difficult to precipitate a coherent image from the sum of the sometimes warring qualities embodied in Wordsworth, Coleridge, Scott, Byron, Keats, Shelley. But established formulae are not so easily cast aside, and even Byron you can find doing an as it were Poets'-Corner-act, even though here the image is only 6 or 8 inches high, and is in the often rather unserious medium of wax. That, however, is what J. Cave, who modelled it in 1835 — well after Byron's death of course — thought poets in general and Byron in particular ought to look like. That Byron would have disapproved trenchantly is certain.

While it is true that certain basic solutions to the problem of indicating the species poet in a portrait of an individual human specimen who happens to be a poet persist, it is also true that between the death of Pope in 1744 and the flowering of the romantics, say from 1790 on, the range of possible variations on these solutions had been enormously enlarged. In England, this was due primarily to the practice and example of Sir Joshua Reynolds, whose great achievement it was to demonstrate in remarkable variety how that most particular craft of likeness-painting could be enlarged to embrace a very general statement. In Reynolds's time the highest branch of painting was acknowledged to be epic or history painting. Reynolds himself longed to excel in that, failed, but managed to raise portraiture, in his best work, to that level. Two examples of his flexibility must serve. The classification of a sitter as a man of letters by including pen and paper in his portrait repeats *ad nauseam*. We have seen a very accomplished but conventional version of it in Van Loo's painting of Pope in 1742 — accomplished it is, but it remains a cliché. Some twelve years later, Reynolds produced his first portrait

94 Byron. Wax, miniature statuette, by J. Cave, 1835

Pl. 73

95 Dr Johnson. By Sir
Joshua Reynolds, 1756

of Samuel Johnson, likewise as man of letters, with pen and paper.
Though not contemplative to the point of leaning head on hand,
Johnson is in reverie. It seems explicit enough, but some time later it
was thought to need further attributes, and a volume of the
dictionary was painted in, plus a rather gratuitous extra quill-cum-
inkpot. These were removed in 1977: if Johnson seems to have got
younger by cleaning, his frown gone, the full corporeal presence of
that massive torso is even more clearly revealed; the expressiveness of

the whole body is ruthlessly individual but the mood is generic —
Samuel Johnson perhaps as poet or perhaps as lexicographer raising
the craft of dictionary-compiling to the level of poetry, intent on the
brink of a perfect definition. In a later portrait, we have Johnson's
face still firmly and unflatteringly characterized, but the portrait as a
whole here cast into a more purely classic and heroic mould, minus
wig and plus toga, a peripatetic philosopher, almost physically
wrenching reason into words. Formally, the pose owes something

96 Dr Johnson. By J.
Watson, 1770, after Sir
Joshua Reynolds

surely to some Italian, perhaps Bolognese, model; or it could read almost as if it were a detail taken from some such epic composition as Raphael's *Disputa* or *School of Athens*.[1]

Unfortunately, Reynolds painted few poets, and his achievement proved to be a peak from which subsequent accomplishment declined. In one charming eccentricity, a theme we have lost sight of for some time was revived by Joseph Wright of Derby in 1781: his portrait of Sir Brooke Boothby has the poet prone by a stream in a woodland glade. Boothby was primarily no doubt a landed gentleman, but also very much a poet himself, associate of Anna Seward, the female Swan of Lichfield. His dress may seem more suitable for circulation in St. James's than rural ramble and meditation on the damp earth: he keeps his gloves on. The book he holds, however, is Rousseau; no doubt the *Juge de Jean-Jacques – Dialogue*, the manuscript of which Rousseau had given to Boothby and Boothby had had published in Lichfield the year before. In spite of the subject's somewhat formal (if prostrate) elegance, the mood is redolent of back-to-nature, echoing indeed sentiments far further back than Rousseau – Milton's *Il Penseroso*, or for example (and

97 Sir Brooke Boothby. By Joseph Wright of Derby, 1781

very closely) James Thomson in *The Seasons* 'Let me haste into the mid-wood shade/And on the dark green grass beside the brink/Of haunted stream . . . lie at large,/And sing the glories of the circling year'.[2] The poet recumbent, however, whom we first sighted in the effigy of John Gower, is perhaps most satisfactorily accommodated in such a memorial function. A variation, the semi-recumbent or reclining posture — reminiscent of that of banqueting Romans, or Etruscans on their tombs — was developed with great success in Tischbein's famous vision of Goethe at much the same time (1786) as Wright's vision of Boothby. Tischbein's portrait, however, while showing the poet draped loosely in a cloak and with 'melancholic' hat, has him sited in the Roman campagna, brooding over antiquity. Though infused with a gentle sensibility that is romantic, it is essentially a neoclassic image: Goethe is thirty-seven, the fervours of *Werther* and *Götz* already ten years behind him.[3]

In England, the mantle of Reynolds passed to the young prodigy, Thomas Lawrence. He could produce results that were literally more brilliant than Reynolds, but in a narrower vein: his portrait of Southey, in 1829, conveys that glint of intelligence and sensibility on a handsome face with which Lawrence as no other could illuminate his sitters. Southey, though, for all that he is placed out of doors, does seem to inhabit nature almost — but perhaps not quite — as if it were a drawing-room; it is perhaps too like a stage set.[4] The greatest — and now rather unjustly neglected — of Scottish portraitists, Raeburn, could do rather better on this sort of theme, and his portrait of 1808 of Sir Walter Scott has indeed been called, owing to its iconography, 'one of the representative images of European romanticism'. Pl. 98

Pl. 99

Raeburn's fault was often to rely too heavily on the use of forced lighting effects on his sitter's features, so that the contrast of light and shade becomes almost melodramatic. Here, if it be held to be melodrama, it is surely justified. The poet is seated in a ruin on a lofty crag; the castle is that called the Hermitage; the mountains of Scotland, distant and inhospitable presences under an ominous sky, are beyond. A fitful shaft of light finds him in a concentration of contemplation that is both internal and externalized in the wild majesty of his setting. Even the dog, almost sunk from sight apart from the pale patch on its breast and the whites of the eyes, seems an attendant familiar rather than a domestic pet.[5] Scott's portraits in fact rival and perhaps surpass those of Pope in quantity, but, with few exceptions of which this is the outstanding one, they are curiously tame, tending to the cosily picturesque: in his oft-repeated marble bust by Chantrey, what in the classical bust should be a toga is chequered into tartan plaid.[6] Pl. 100

A number of his portraits do, though, refer to specific new interests of the romantic era — locally, to a new intensity of pride in

98 Southey. By Sir Thomas
Lawrence, 1829

the Scottish past, and more generally, to the picturesque of the
Middle Ages and British history. In this the bust of Shakespeare
inevitably played its part. Veneration of Shakespeare's person had
continued of course – the painting of Garrick's protégé, the actor

Pl. 101   William Powell, grouped with his family about a bust of the Bard, is
but one eloquent witness to that. 'Never let your Shakespeare be out
of your hands . . . keep him about you as a charm,' Garrick had
written to Powell. That painting, by J. H. Mortimer, is of some time
back, in 1768,[7] but the mode of devotion persisted much later, as is

Pl. 104   evident in Flaxman's design for the memorial plaque to the
Shakespearian editor, George Steevens, of 1800 (recently salvaged
from the decay of St. Matthias's Church, Poplar). If the bust of
Shakespeare here is of rather uncertain derivation, and in hair-style

99 Sir Walter Scott. By Sir
Henry Raeburn, 1808

and doublet markedly unclassical, of the classic pose and demeanour
of his devotee there can be no argument,[8] while the small change of
the circulation of Shakespeare's image kept often to an image that is
positively Grecian in atmosphere, like the cameo medallions
produced by the firm of Wedgwood in some quantity over a long
period.

Pls. 102 and 103

There was, though, a growing fascination, from about 1800
onwards, in historical portraits: a desire for authentic contemporary
likenesses of the great historical figures of the past rather than
idealized heroic re-creations. This reflects an antiquarian urge — one
that was very close to Walter Scott's heart — and an emotional, often
sentimental, romantic involvement, the authentic portrait assuming
the aura of sympathetic magic of the relic.

100 (*right*) Sir Walter Scott.
By Sir Francis Chantrey.
Dated 1841; one of many
repetitions of a bust for
which Scott sat in the 1820s

101 (*below*) William Powell.
By J. H. Mortimer, 1768

102 (*above left*) Shakespeare.
Wedgwood medallion

103 (*above right*) Shakespeare.
Wedgwood basalt bust

104 (*left*) George Steevens.
By J. Flaxman, 1800

105 Sir Walter Scott. By Sir
William Allan, 1832

So it is that in Sir William Allan's portrait of Scott in his study in
1832, there appears — amongst the medieval paraphernalia, armour,
and so on — on the mantelpiece, not a classicizing bust of
Shakespeare, but a literal cast of the real thing, the figure from the
monument at Stratford-upon-Avon. Allied to that is a rather
touching painting of Scott recently acquired by the Shakespeare
Birthplace Trust at Stratford: the painter is unknown, but the style is
very close again to Sir William Allan. Scott is shown brooding in
meditation at the edge of Shakespeare's grave in Holy Trinity,
Stratford, with the bust glimmering in the wall above. Haydon has
been suggested as the painter of this, but unhappily it is on stylistic
grounds very unlikely — unhappily, because Haydon catches the

106 Sir Walter Scott. By an
unidentified artist, at
Shakespeare's grave,
Stratford-upon-Avon

mood of the effigy ('his simple and unaffected Bust') and its setting so
exactly in words, recording in his Diary his own visit of July 1828:
'the most poetical imagination could not have imagined a burial
place more worthy, more suitable, more English, more native for a
Poet than this, and above all for Shakespeare! . . . I would not barter
[that] simple, sequestered tomb in Stratford for the Troad, the
Acropolis, or the field of Marathon.'[9]

I used the word 'glimmering' perhaps rather fancifully of the
monument at Stratford, but that in fact was what it was doing in
1828 and had been since 1793, when the austere taste of one of the

greatest of Shakespearian scholars, Malone, was offended by its
colouring. Malone held that sculpture should be monochrome, as he
believed, if wrongly, that all classical statuary had been. The colour,
he thought, was a barbarous innovation of a known restoration
exercise on the bust in 1749. So he got it whitewashed, and so it
remained until 1861 when the colour was revealed. The documentation of the bust by reproduction is a troubled subject that I do not
propose to become involved in here in any detail. As we have
observed earlier, it was known to the world at large in the
seventeenth century only by the travesty reproduced in Dugdale's
Warwickshire. In the 1720s Pope, in his edition of Shakespeare,
offered a new reproduction, an engraving by Vertue. This is more
credible as a reproduction of a possible piece of monumental
statuary, but for reasons unknown Vertue – although he knew
Stratford – has substituted a head based closely on the Chandos
portrait of Shakespeare for the head that was actually there. Then in
1749 there was a restoration, and in 1793 Malone's whitewashing.
This confusion has begotten a dreadful shelf-full of polemical
literature of charge and countercharge:[10] that the effigy now at
Stratford is, is not, a replacement, or outright fake. I will only say
here that I am perfectly convinced that the monument is that
recorded by the First Folio as *in situ* by 1623,[11] though the relation of
its present colouring to the original colouring may well not be
entirely accurate. The repetition of it that Scott had on his
mantelpiece anyway reflected Malone's drastic views about desirable
pallor for statuary, and was probably one of the many monochrome
casts that one George Bullock produced from a mould of the effigy in
1814. This version was also broadcast to a still wider public by
engravings, now showing a faithful literal reproduction of the effigy
but, of course, indicating that it was without colouring.

Pl. 108

Pl. 107

The demand for the authentic was liable to betrayal by other
things than whitewash. The tendency of the market, when a
significant demand for anything makes itself felt, is to manufacture to
meet the demand. The output of engravings, mainly derivative at
various distances from the Chandos portrait of Shakespeare, increased steadily from the late eighteenth century through the
nineteenth. But engravings are reproductions, and so are casts, not
quite the real thing; to supply the need for that, more originals were
necessary. The industry of fake Shakespeares only got going in mass
in the nineteenth century;[12] I shall offer a rigorously selective choice
of a few specimens in that output later on, but there are fakes and
fakes. Some of the later, 100 per cent ones, are original creations of a
sort not entirely devoid of eccentric charm, but of course there are
simpler ways of producing a new portrait of Shakespeare than by
doing the whole thing from scratch. One can simply label a genuine

portrait of an unknown man of the period that one thinks, innocently or with intent to deceive for profit, looks like Shakespeare, as Shakespeare. A miniature owned by the Earl of Oxford as early as 1719 was called Shakespeare, and even got engraved as him for Pope's edition of the *Works* in 1721; it is clearly not Shakespeare, though it is an authentic image of the period of someone who looked more like Drake than Shakespeare. Whether it was innocently rebaptized or not is uncertain, but a contemporary considered it had been 'palmed upon Mr Pope for an original', while Oxford – as we have noted earlier – certainly owned also a poet's portrait that is the earliest demonstrable example of faking a genuine portrait of one person to look like another – Fuller's painting, now in the Tate, that Oxford acquired as of the poet Cleveland but which cleaning has proved to be of an unknown architect (see p. 63).

A rather different approach is to alter an existing portrait of someone else to look like what you think Shakespeare ought to look like. That technique has indeed been applied to Shakespeare, and the earliest example of it in his case has proved to have a remarkable stamina, widely known, reproduced and copied through the nineteenth century and still not all that rarely reproduced today as Shakespeare without query. It surfaced around 1770, and is known as

107 (*left*) Shakespeare. From a plaster cast (monochrome) by George Bullock, 1814

108 (*right*) Shakespeare. The Stratford monument, as engraved by G. Vertue, 1721

Pl. 109

109 'Shakespeare'. By
George Vertue, 1721

110 'Shakespeare'. Painting
(the 'Janssen portrait') of (?)
Sir Thomas Overbury
adjusted to resemble
Shakespeare

the 'Janssen' portrait;[13] it now resides in that fabulous repository of Shakespeariana, the Folger Library at Washington. It is basically a perfectly genuine portrait of the period, in the manner of Janssen, that is Cornelius Johnson, but doubts, expressed notably by the most scrupulous student of Shakespeare portraiture, M. H. Spielmann, were for me confirmed definitively by the appearance of another version of it in a London saleroom.[14] As is quite clear from comparison of the two, the 'Janssen' version has been modulated into Shakespeare by simply pushing back the hair-line till the brow approximates to the famous dome that is the common factor of the two fully authenticated portraits as also of the Chandos painting. The unaltered version was sold as of an unknown man, but an earlier inventory of the Ellenborough family collection, from which it came, lists a portrait of Sir Thomas Overbury that is later unaccounted for. If one compares the unaltered version of the 'Janssen' with the fully authenticated portrait of 1613 of Overbury[15] in the Bodleian Library, the conclusion that in the other 'Janssen' Sir Thomas Overbury, the well-known central figure in a notorious Jacobean poisoning case, is being masqueraded as Shakespeare seems convincing. I do not suppose either would have been pleased. But the 'Janssen' image persisted in live flesh and blood even in the 1970s: the actor Tim Curry, playing Shakespeare, appeared dressed and made up as a facsimile of it.[16]

Pl. 110

Pl. 111

Pl. 112

111 (*left*) Sir Thomas Overbury(?). Artist unknown

112 (*right*) Sir Thomas Overbury. Artist unknown, 1613

SHAKESPEARE · SACRIFICED; · or _ The Offering to AVARICE.

113 'Shakespeare Sacrificed'.
By James Gillray, 1789

Apart from the search for the authentic likeness, with all its hazards, there is of course no reason why a demand for imaginary portraits should not continue, though one would expect them to be no longer, as I have already indicated, necessarily in a classical heroic mode, but rather conjured up in the mood and weather of the romantic imagination. In fact, the happiest examples of these retain in form the visual glamour of neoclassicism, but softened in that frequent, and frequently very engaging, meld of neoclassic form with romantic sensibility. Around 1786, Alderman Boydell got under way the ambitious project called his 'Shakespeare Gallery'. This venture had interlinked aims: to pay visual homage to Shakespeare; to inspire with national themes a new school of English history painters, as so ardently desired by Sir Joshua Reynolds; and to recoup Boydell financially by means of a heavily promoted sale of engravings of the pictures.[17] The whole exercise was seen by the caricaturist James Gillray as a sell-out to blatant commercialism; in 1789, in the month after Boydell's Gallery was opened in Pall Mall, Gillray published a savage attack on it in his print *Shakespeare – Sacrificed – or – The Offering to Avarice*, displayed no doubt in the window of Mrs Humphrey's print-shop just up the road, in the

Pl. 113

Haymarket. Folly fans a pyre of the plays into flame, and the smoke is peopled by travesties from some of the paintings in Boydell's Gallery. The statue (Scheemakers's) of Shakespeare is shrouded in the smoke.[18]

The subjects represented in Boydell's Gallery were of course not portraits of Shakespeare but subjects taken from the plays, and the only paintings that had anything to do with Shakespeare's portraiture were rather unorthodox. Inspired by a passage from Gray's *Progress of Poesy*, George Romney experimented with several variations on the theme of natural genius in the form of a new-born child being tended, its end even being shaped, by supranatural forces: it is a train of thought that no doubt stems at some distance from the Christian theme of the adoration of the Christ Child, from classical images such as the Infant Hercules, and at a rather less remote remove perhaps from a strange painting by Sir Joshua Reynolds believed to represent Dr Samuel Johnson as a singular heavyweight highbrow babe.[19] Romney's cartoon, now in the Walker Art Gallery in Liverpool, of about 1786 (though the design exists in other versions and variants) shows Nature unveiling the Infant Shakespeare, with Comedy and Tragedy attendant in devotion. The actual 'sitter' was the child of a handy guardsman.[20] The theme evidently found an answering chord at the time, and some twenty years later (in 1805) Fuseli produced a more sinister and demonic variation, though this

Pl. 114

114 (*left*) Nature unveiling the Infant Shakespeare. Cartoon, by George Romney, *c.*1786(?)

115 (*right*) 'The Infant Shakespeare'. By H. Fuseli, 1805

116 Shakespeare and the
Muses. Sculptured pediment,
by Thomas Banks, 1789, engraved by B. Smith, 1796

time it becomes almost a parody of one of the most popular themes
of the eighteenth century, Hercules confronted by the choice at the
crossroads: a theme that Reynolds again had restated in a famous and
brilliant painting of Garrick between the rival claims of Comedy and
Tragedy. Here Fuseli has the Infant Shakespeare being suckled by
Tragedy but tempted by Comedy.[21] Fuseli was much involved with
Boydell's Shakespeare Gallery but he conceived an alternative of
his own, a Milton Gallery, and the potent image of the Miltonic
Lucifer, the fallen angel as hero, is already there moving towards its
definition in the Byronic myth.

Pl. 116
There was one other image of Shakespeare involved in the
Boydell venture. It was not a painting but a sculpture in a high relief
incorporated originally in the pediment of Boydell's Gallery in Pall
Mall where the paintings were exhibited. It was removed thence
following the bankruptcy of the project, and can now be found in the
garden of New Place at Stratford. It looks somewhat forlorn there,
but in its time one critic saluted its sculptor, Thomas Banks, for

117 'Shakespeare in the midst of his creations'. By Henry Howard, *c.*1829(?)

having produced in it 'the most perfect piece of sculpture yet made by an Englishman'.[22] Whatever a current view of that may be, it is a little odd to reflect that the sculptor of the Stratford effigy, Johnson, and all three sculptors who attended subsequently to the Shakespearian theme – Scheemakers, Rysbrack, and Roubiliac – had indeed been foreign-born. Here the poet – shown as adult of course, though clad in costume nearer the Van Dyckian romantic of Scheemakers and Roubiliac – is conceived in terms close to the neoclassic in handling, iconography, and sentiment; he is supported in his questing gaze for inspiration by the Muses of Painting and Drama. In fact, I think the high ranking suggested for it, by the critic quoted, in the annals of English sculpture is scarcely justified; few would be inclined to include it in the best work even of its maker, Banks himself, for his very original, powerful, and skilful talent produced images far more compelling. But even so, when one comes to look for the full-bloodedly romantic embodiment of the spirit of Shakespeare in the sort of a shape one might, if naively, expect to find it, it is to be disappointed. There is no worthy equivalent of Raeburn's Walter Scott. A precursor of romantic criticism, Felton, in his *Imperfect Hints towards a New Edition of Shakespeare* of 1787, remarks that 'the magic of [Shakespeare's] muse had bodied forth things unknown, and he has transfixed a portion of that divine spirit which nature gave him, to airy nothings — to whom he has given a charm that will never fade . . .' Though that may perhaps seem to identify in the poet a power of fancy rather than of imagination, it does contain the concept of imagination divinely inspired reigning over reason. The only equivalent involving Shakespeare's person that comes to mind hovers on the brink of collapse from sublimity to Pl. 117   ridiculousness — Henry Howard's painting of about 1829 of Shakespeare resting in the lap of Fancy contemplating the visions (Howard called it 'Shakespeare in the midst of his creations') that she conjures up.

That is not a picture that late twentieth-century taste finds easy to accept as being even seriously intended. Yet it was accepted as such, and indeed hangs still where its first owner put it, in that odd little shrine of Shakespeariana off the stairs in Sir John Soane's house in Lincoln's Inn Fields, now the Soane Museum. It is accompanied by one of Bullock's pale monochrome casts of the Stratford effigy, and the whole little temple, almost chapel, alcove is a strange survivor of some of the absorptions of the early nineteenth century. But in the end, the most satisfactory of romantic reinterpretations of Shakespeare in portrait comes from a source not normally associated with portraits — William Blake.

About 1800, William Hayley commissioned from Blake a set of portraits of poets for his library at Felpham.[23] Blake's usual — one cannot say normal — idiom when summoning up the spirits of the past, Newton or Milton, was far from literal, reflecting more the mood of his own interior visions, as on the Sussex shore for this commission he communed with the spirits of the poets: 'All majestic shadows, grey but luminous, and superior to the common height of man'. In his long dialogues with the shade of Dante he did maintain recognizably that hatchet profile that cleaves its way through the centuries with such authority, but only once, amongst the portraits for Hayley's library (now all in Manchester City Art Gallery), did he Pl. 118   portray Shakespeare. For Shakespeare, he restated the Droeshout engraving from the Folios, and is indeed one of the few to have expressed approval of that image. But though it is executed in grisaille, almost colourless, it is both a fine humanization and haunting spiritualization of it, 'grey but luminous' as he had seen the spirits of the poets, and wreathed not in conventional ivy, laurel, or bays but in flowering convolvulus, with the armoured shade of Macbeth on one side confronted by the three witches and the ghost

118 Shakespeare. By
William Blake, *c.*1800

of the murdered Banquo pointing to the apparition of the eight
kings, though only one of them is visible.

Blake's own portraits – the portraits of him – offer an engaging
illustration of the two extremes of poets' portraiture, with two
different and novel elements added in, one of them arising from his
status as an original visual artist of genius concomitant with that of a
poet of genius. At the one extreme, the informal likeness – the
record of a man, of a friend, for friendship's sake, how he looked, the
actual shape and costume in which he occupied space and time in his
time – Blake was affectionately and credibly served by two young
disciples: most often in a number of quite informal studies by John
Linnell, but also by George Richmond. Two examples must serve.
One is inscribed on the back later by Linnell: 'Mr Blake on the hill
before our cottage at Hampstead *c.*1825 I guess';[24] the other is dated
by Linnell as 1820.[25] Both then show Blake in his old age, the former
only two years before he died in 1827. (There seems to be nothing of
Blake of any literal value before he was about forty-six.) Both equate
happily with Samuel Palmer's memory of Blake as 'a man without a
mask: his aim single, his path straightforwards, and his wants few: so
he was free, noble and happy. His voice and manner were quiet, yet
all awake with intellect . . .' No hint of the madness, with which
contemporary opinion endowed him, appears, but nor does much of
the passion, violence even, of some of his poetry and the invective of
his comment. His costume is entirely conventional, only the eyes
seem large and with perhaps a possibility of apocalypse in their
openness: the finest eye that Samuel Palmer ever saw, he noted,

Pl. 119

Pl. 120

119 Blake. By John Linnell,
c.1820

120 Blake. By John Linnell,
c.1825

121 Blake. By Thomas Phillips, 1807

Pl. 121

'brilliant but not roving, clear and intent, yet susceptible; it flashed with genius, or melted with tenderness. It could also be terrible.' At the other end of the gamut of representation is the well-known painting, life-scale, by Thomas Phillips, in the National Portrait Gallery.[26] Considerably earlier, painted in 1807, it is an entirely competent but conventional formula of the poet as poet or artist, pen in hand – eyes upwards to whatever source of inspiration, the body simultaneously turned slightly away as if almost in apprehension of that inspiration (just as conventionally the Virgin is shown recoiling from the Angel of the Annunciation). This is as it were the expected image of the poet, and as such reproduced frequently through the nineteenth century. Remembering Blake after his death in piety,

122 Blake. By George
Richmond

Pl. 122   even George Richmond, who had produced one rough but sturdily
convincing sketch[27] of Blake standing whole-length, *ad vivum* in his
everyday habit, could feel impelled to grope towards the ideal image
Pl. 123   in a profile design.[28] This was much later, about 1857, remembering — twenty years after the poet's death — and transposing him
now into a design that is so close to one of Kneller's of Alexander
Pl. 64   Pope that it is hard to believe he did not have it consciously or
subconsciously in mind: the classic profile.

The novel elements, though, in Blake's portraits stem from two
sources — his self-portraits, if such they be, in the first case. One is
Pl. 124   peculiar:[29] it comes from the Blake/Varley Sketchbook of Visionary
Heads, and the suggestion is that it is Blake's rejection of and
counterblast to a somewhat insipid version of a profile of him used by
Varley for a publication called *Zodiacal Physiognomy* — not published
till 1828, though this drawing appears to be of 1819. Allegedly it
represents Blake as the type of person born under Cancer. Literally, it
exaggerates the bulge of brow and stare of eye, while accentuating at
least a snubness of nose, a quality on which Blake was wont to
comment fondly; it has been called a self-caricature. It is perhaps a
Pl. 125   self-distortion in the direction of a caricature, just as another one[30] is
a self-distortion far on the way to ideal self-portraiture, or, more
truly than the first, a 'visionary head'. The subject of this became

123 (*above left*) Blake. By
George Richmond, *c.*1857

124 (*above right*) Blake.
'Self-caricature', 1819

125 (*left*) Blake. (?)Visionary
self-portrait, *c.*1820

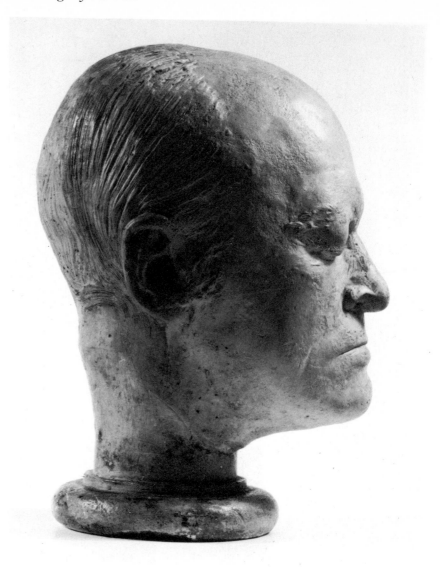

126 & 127 Blake. Life-
mask, taken by J. S. Deville,
1823 (a) Profile (b) Full-face

confused, and it was known as 'Lais of Corinth, the Courtesan', but
two copies or tracings of it by Linnell were inscribed as *The Portrait of
a Man who instructed Mr Blake in Painting, etc. in his Dreams*, and the
suggestion is that Blake received instruction in dreams from a
visionary version of himself, here delineated in an enigmatic flame-
like characterization, the ornament pendant on his forehead being
based on the menorah, a symbol of spiritual enlightenment, its
significance here heightened by its place in the central area on the
forehead, in Indian yoga a major centre of meditation, or 'third eye'.

    The 'visionary head' is generally dated about 1820: its relation to
the physical mass of Blake's head of flesh and blood is perhaps not
more, or less, than that of the flame lambent on the coal. That one can

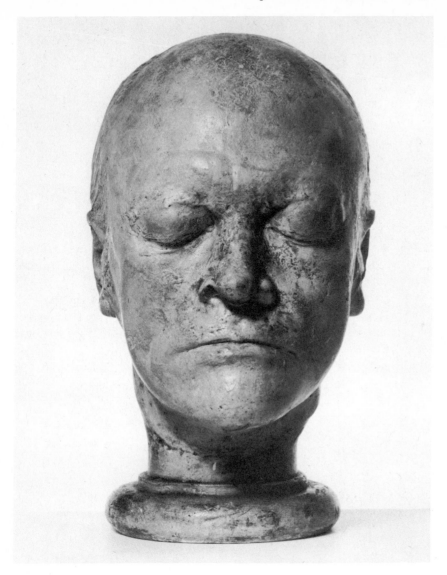

test against the magnificent version of the second new kind of poet's
portrait, the life mask that J. S. Deville made of Blake in 1823.[31]
Deville was a professional maker of moulds and casts, and also an
amateur phrenologist, a pseudo-science allied to physiognomy then
enjoying a considerable boom. Blake's head is said to have been taken
as an example 'representative of the imaginative faculty'; as object, I
personally find it one of the most satisfactory of poets' portraits, not
only because it literally is, in its physical dimension, the poet, but also
because Blake seems to have been such a satisfactory incarnation of
himself. Putting it another way, it is a refutation for once of Max
Beerbohm's often quoted and indeed often justifiable complaint that
so few people look like themselves. It is of course a rather dour

Pls. 126 and 127

version of Blake who dearly loved a laugh, owing no doubt to the oppressive technique of taking such masks, the face (and apparently in this unique case the entire head) being swaddled in wet plaster, with lifelines provided by two straws up the nostrils. But what a marvellous object, infinitely more numinous for me than a visionary head, yet its reality emphasized by the febrile variations that two celebrated artists of the twentieth century, Epstein and Bacon, have performed on its theme, Bacon returning to it again and again in a series of versions.[32] Two original casts survive, the first being probably that now in the Fitzwilliam Museum.

Fortunately life masks of two more of the major British romantic poets have survived, owing, however, not to phrenological curiosity on Deville's part but to a more abstract and heroic interest in proportion on the part of that heroic, frenzied, and doomed painter, Benjamin Robert Haydon. When Wordsworth sat to him, Haydon was enchanted to find him 'to my wonder, eight heads high, or five feet $9\frac{7}{8}$ inches, and of very fine heroic proportions'. Haydon's life mask of Keats,[33] taken in December 1816, is the equal of the Blake in its fittingness for its subject, seeming in the dreaming delicacy of its strength, its eager yet serene clarity, the ideal figure-head for the finest of his poetry. It makes the 'art-portraits' of him seem coarse and

Pl. 128

128 (*right*) Keats. Life-mask taken by B. R. Haydon, December 1816

129 (*far right*) Keats. By B. R. Haydon, 1816

130 Keats. Small-scale painting (posthumous), by J.
Severn

clumsy; devoted as his friend Severn undoubtedly was, his portraits
of the poet have mainly sentimental value, while the well-known
whole-length of Keats seated in that attitude of poetic melancholy   Pl. 130
that we have seen so often was painted posthumously, and both the
head and the hand — the latter especially, painted from a cast — seem
indeed dead, as if snapped in a waxwork exhibition. That is in spite of
Severn's claim that it really is 'the last pleasant remembrance' of the
poet, when visiting him on the day he had written the 'Ode to a
Nightingale'. 'The room, the open window, the carpet, chairs are all
exact portraits, even to the mezzotint portrait of Shakespeare given
him by his old landlady, in the Isle of Wight . . .'(which type of
engraving — though surely a Chandos derivative — is not, however,
quite clear, though Keats would have at least approved the presence
of his 'Presider'; see below, p. 148).[34] Haydon did better than   Pl. 129
Severn not only in the life mask but also in quick pen-and-ink
impressions of the profile,[35] and he included faces based both on
Wordsworth and on Keats in a religious composition.

131 (*left*) Coleridge. By P. Vandyke, 1795

132 (*right*) Coleridge. By Washington Allston, 1814

Pl. 131

Pl. 132

Keats died aged only twenty-six; the chance that perpetuated such vivid likeness as the mask and Haydon's drawings was fortunate indeed. The cases of the great founder figures, Wordsworth and Coleridge, are less happy. The early portraits of Coleridge are mere likenesses.[36] That by P. Vandyke, of 1795, presents a youth of perhaps unexpected, almost pretty, elegance, but it does not rise much above a likeness; nor does that by a much more accomplished painter, James Northcote, recently acquired by Jesus College, Cambridge, but painted originally for that great patron of poetry, as of painting, of his time, Sir George Beaumont, in 1804. This is capable and yet rather inert. One expects too much of course; Northcote himself once confessed sadly that a portrait is only a little better as a memorial than the parings of the nails or a lock of hair. Another portraitist of Coleridge, Washington Allston, painting him in 1814, striving to kindle some kind of romantic atmospherics by this Gothick setting, reflected on his failure later: 'So far as I can judge . . . the likeness is a true one. But it is Coleridge in repose, and though not unstirred by the perpetual groundswell of his ever-working intellect . . . it is not Coleridge in his highest state – the poetic mood. When in that state no face I ever saw was like his, it seemed almost spirit made visible, without a shadow of the visible upon it . . . But it was beyond the reach of my art.'[37] And indeed

133 Wordsworth. By H. Meyer, 1819, after R. Carruthers, 1817

that presence did escape all those who tried to paint Coleridge and is best glimpsed now as it were between the lines of the poetry and the notebooks, and in a few verbal descriptions of rare felicity, especially perhaps Hazlitt's memory of first meeting him. It is a pity indeed that Hazlitt's painting of Coleridge has not survived. One or two of Hazlitt's rare surviving portraits — and he trained as a professional painter — notably that of Charles Lamb, suggest that his Coleridge might have been rewarding. On the other hand, his Wordsworth, likewise done at the same time and likewise lost, seems not to have been appreciated; it was described by a friend as looking as 'if at the gallows — deeply affected by his deserved fate — yet determined to die like a man'. Hazlitt, though, did think Wordsworth his ideal of 'physiognomical perfection'. As I have noted, Haydon thought something rather similar, and wrote too of Wordsworth's look being a man 'conscious of a high calling', his only equal in that being Keats. For us now, once we start collating the great profusion of portraits of Wordsworth,[38] the grounds for this assessment may seem confused. A plethora there certainly is — rivalling Pope and Scott in quantity — but unfortunately the very few witnesses of him in anything approaching youth are incompetent, dreary, and void. The first image of him to gain wide circulation was by a rather obscure artist called R. Carruthers, only in 1817 when Wordsworth   Pl. 133

134 Wordsworth. Drawing,
life-scale, by B. R. Haydon,
1817

was already forty-seven, and near twenty years after the first
publication of the *Lyrical Ballads*.[39] Engravings of it were popular,
but it was a very conventional exercise, and indeed, like Richmond's
Blake, so close to a portrait of Pope by Kneller, though another one
(that of 1722, Pl. 67) than Richmond's, as to be almost startling: the
poet melancholic, head on hand. It provoked an odd comment from
de Quincey, who maintained that one of Jonathan Richardson's
engravings of Milton (Blanshard, *Wordsworth*, pl. 19b) was a closer
likeness of Wordsworth than Carruthers's portrait of him. However,
Haydon, so often maligned as painter, in Wordsworth's case did
have a success,[40] and his vision of Wordsworth by no means entirely
betrays his estimate of Wordsworth's genius. The sitter thought it
'the best likeness, that is the most characteristic, which has been done
of me'. Seen brooding on Helvellyn, in 1842, the poet may seem to

Pl. 135

135 Wordsworth. By B. R. Haydon, 1842

be making rather heavy weather of it all, but it is one of the few worthy paintings of the English romantic poets: as with Raeburn's Scott, the weather and the mood are in fact right. Elizabeth Barrett closes her sonnet on it with: 'This is the poet and his poetry.' Haydon's much earlier drawing of Wordsworth,[41] in 1818, perhaps overstates the case, and the mood there verges on the Byronic – though to the perhaps misleading associations of the fashion of the open-necked shirt we shall come in a moment. Likewise the life mask,[42] taken for Haydon in the Lake District even earlier (1815), and transported down to London, fails for some reason to have the impact of the mask of either Keats or Blake: it seems to me curiously very much a mask veiling rather than unveiling. It remained for the most fashionable sculptor of the age, Sir Francis Chantrey, in a marble bust[43] of 1820, when Wordsworth was fifty, to justify

Pl. 134

Pl. 137

Pl. 136

others' impressions of 'physiognomical perfection' or heroic pro-portions in Wordsworth's person. Commissioned by Sir George Beaumont, it is in the persistent neoclassic idiom, the stray lock of hair on the forehead providing perhaps a sole specific romantic accent: some may think it over-prettified, over-smooth, but for me it seems just what the ideal bust in marble should be for such a subject. Coleridge said of it that it was more like Wordsworth than Wordsworth was like himself (though that could be a double-edged comment). In contrast, the average portraits of him in the later years of his life, apart from Haydon's, seem trite and almost impertinent. Pickersgill's painting[44] in the National Portrait Gallery (a whole-length variation, perhaps posthumous, of an earlier original of 1832–3 in St. John's College, Cambridge) is better than most, yet is tame and shows the poet tamed.

136 (*left*) Wordsworth. By Sir F. Chantrey, 1820

137 (*right*) Wordsworth. Life-mask, taken by B. R. Haydon, 1815

138 Wordsworth. By H. W. Pickersgill, *c.* 1850–1, the head based on a portrait of 1832–3

The poet who was never tamed was of course Byron. Though it was for his thirty-sixth birthday that he wrote

> My days are in the yellow leaf;
>   The flowers and fruits of love are gone;
> The worm, the canker, and the grief
>   Are mine alone!

and his physical beauty and health were perhaps already shattered, he qualifies for ever amongst those whom the Gods love and who die young, even if the Gods' love be something of a love-hatred in his provocative case. When he died at Missolonghi that same year, a whole nation, Greece, went into mourning, and all over Europe the echo of his death reverberated as no other death of the time except Napoleon's. And it was in the light of such exalted comparisons that his physical presence was seen.[45] 'Lord Byron's head', wrote Lockhart, 'is without doubt the finest in our time. I think it better on the whole, than either Napoleon's, or Goethe's, or Canova's, or Wordsworth's.'

It was also Lockhart (later son-in-law of Walter Scott) who in 1821 in a defence of *Don Juan* wrote that 'nobody could have written it but a man of the first order both in genius and in dissipation — a real master of all his tools, a profligate, pernicious, irresistible, charming, Devil . . .' That may serve as reminder of the nature of the Byronic hero that shocked and hypnotized Europe, and has been the subject of a continuing learned and international commentary ever since. My concern is with the physical stock from which the legend sprang or on to which it was grafted, but it is odd that no one has yet compiled the necessary source-book to enable one to do so with full confidence. A number of articles in magazines have been published over the years, but there is no monograph on the portraits of Byron, though there is a book, a monograph, or a learned article, or several, on almost any other aspect of that extraordinary human phenomenon that you can think of. The impact of his actual work on that of his British and European contemporaries, and his relationship with them, are endlessly discussed; perhaps less frequently but frequently enough are discussed also the character and spread of Byronic man and his view of the world, a view illustrated in the visual and musical arts as illustriously as in literature. Berlioz transposed his spirit into music, and Delacroix was the greatest interpreter in painting — but never met Byron and never painted him, though there is a self-portrait of Delacroix as Hamlet already in 1821 that could almost be a portrait of Byron as Manfred or vice versa,[46] while Courbet's patron, Bruyas, owned a portrait said to be Byron, by Géricault.[47]

The earliest portrait of any importance and authenticity is that by

George Sanders, begun in 1807 and apparently commissioned by the
nineteen-year-old Byron himself, painted for his mother and now in
the Royal Collection.[48] It may relate to an actual project of a
Scottish tour to conclude with a voyage to the Western Isles, but to
hindsight seems both prophetic of what was to come and a fairly
compendious image of what the young Byron ought to look like. It
suggests a restless independence, high impetuousness combined with
a certain hesitation of mood. Dark sea, stormy sky, and craggy cliffs
could well illustrate, say, *The Corsair.* Its author, George Sanders, was
a Scottish painter (now obscure), with ambitions in oil-painting
which were never fully answered. This is certainly his masterpiece,
and, as engraved as the only illustration to Moore's biography of
Byron (1830), it became an enduring definition of the image of the
young Byron. For his living, though, Sanders depended on
miniatures, and there seem to have been at least two by him of
Byron, one or both existing in several versions: their dating and
interrelationship is still uncertain (but between 1810 and 1812), as is
Byron's own reaction to them. He certainly disapproved strongly of
the engraving of one of them, and forbade its appearance in a new
edition of *Childe Harold* in 1812.[49] He registered disapproval
anyway on principle of a portrait frontispiece — 'the frontispiece of
an author's visage is but a paltry exhibition.'[50] Of the oil-painting,
he thought it did not flatter him, 'but the subject is a bad one . . .' — an
opinion not shared by his mother — 'the countenance is angelic and
the finest I ever saw and it is very like. Miss Rumbold . . . fell quite in
love with it.'[51] Miss Rumbold of course had both predecessors and
many, many successors in that emotion in relation to the original of
the portrait.

Pl. 139

Pl. 140

The miniatures were designed as keepsakes, reminders for friends
to keep in absence of the original: the equivalent of the photograph.
After Byron in 1812 woke one morning — in the famous phrase — to
find himself famous, on the publication of *Childe Harold*, the more
public images became almost inevitable. In 1813/14, he sat to the
fashionable academician, Thomas Phillips, who produced two
different portraits of him, of each of which subsequently a number of
copies were made. They have received on the whole not a very good
press, but nevertheless they have both prevailed on posterity, aided
most notably, I suppose, by the presence and availability of a version
of one of them in the National Portrait Gallery. Hobhouse thought
the likeness was bad; Hazlitt, who saw them when they were both
shown (the sitter unnamed, but known to all) at the Royal Academy
in 1814, was, I guess, near the mark: 'too smooth, and seem, as it
were, "barbered ten times o'er" — there is however much that
conveys the softness and wildness of character of the popular poet of

139 Byron. Painting (small scale), by George Sanders, 1807

140 Byron. Miniature, by
George Sanders, c.1810–12

141 Byron. From a minia-
ture by J. Holmes, 1815

142 Byron. By Thomas
Phillips, 1813–14

Pl. 142

the East.' A quality of 'softness' as diagnosed by Hazlitt would not
have appealed to Byron, but does seem to be there, and especially in
the portrait in Albanian dress. This has always had for me a very
unconvincing whiff of fancy-dress ball, or of Hollywood spectacular, almost Errol Flynn playing Byron. It is of course literally fancy
dress though also authentic, as the costume (strictly 'Arnauot' rather
than Albanian, a specific Albanian tribe) had been bought by Byron
on the Epirus in 1809. The moustache is either strengthened with
dark shading – Byron's beard, when visible, was auburn to flaxen in
colour – or, I think more like, pure burnt cork. It has nevertheless
been described recently 'as the image of Byron's public *persona* in the
period of *The Corsair* and *Lara* – There was in him a vital scorn of

143 Byron. By Thomas
Phillips, 1813–14

all: / As if the worst had fall'n which could befall, / He stood a
stranger in this breathing world. / An erring spirit from another
world.' Seen thus (that assessment goes on), in 'the character [which
is] Byron's most important single contribution to the culture of
Western Europe, the modern type of Fallen Angel, excluded from
human society by having dared to know too much, and regarding
remorse stoically as an aspect of wisdom.'[52] The dark-cloaked
variation of Thomas Phillips's vision of him seems to answer the
needs of that account better than the Albanian one, but neither of   Pl. 143
course captures that unique amalgam of Hero and Anti-Hero that
was Byron. The proper painter, I have suggested, should have been
Delacroix, but if it had to be an English one, it is a pity that Lawrence
did not paint Byron. Like Phillips, he would probably have barbered
the poet somewhat, but would have been more brilliant, more sharp,
and was capable of catching something, if perhaps a rather stagey
something, of the demonic on occasions. He did in fact leave a verbal
description – 'the forehead clear and open, the brow bold and
prominent, the Eye bright and *dissimilar*: the Nose finely cut and the
Nostril *acutely* formed – the Mouth well-formed but wide, and
contemptuous even in its smile; falling singularly at the corners, and
its vindictive and disdainful expression heightened by the massive
firmness of the Chin . . .'[53] But descriptions of Byron are legion and

contradictory. That useful if over-used shorthand word 'charisma' was not about in his day, but if anyone ever had it, it was he; one of its qualities is that of dazzling the beholder, so that verbal impressions of Byron range all the way from Lawrence's to Lady Caroline Lamb's 'That beautiful pale face is my fate' to Lady Hester Stanhope's 'a great deal of vice in his looks – his eyes set close together and a contracted brow. . .' to Claire Clairmont's 'the wild originality of your countenance'. And countless more, all to be read while remembering Byron's own realization of failure to impress a young American fan in 1821 who, thought Byron, 'expected to meet a misanthropical gentleman, in wolf-skin breeches, and answering in fierce monosyllables, instead of a man of this world. I can never get people to understand that poetry is the expression of *excited passion*, and there is no such thing as a life of passion any more than a continuous earthquake, or an eternal fever. Besides, who could ever *shave* themselves in such a state . . .'

144 Byron. By R. Westall,

Nevertheless, the portrait takers continued in their efforts to catch the spirit within the physical form. The year before Phillips, in 1813, Richard Westall had had a shot at Byron, and one that proved, via engravings and copies, perhaps even more influential than Phillips's. It is a variation on the classic topos of poetic melancholy, head on hand, that we have seen so often. The role of working poet is not, however, further spelled out by attributes of pen, paper, and inkpot. Those perhaps, for such an aristocratic subject — though also a true professional if ever there was one — might have smacked almost of trade, while here very notable is that gaze diverted from the spectator, aloof and self-proposed for admiration, especially as here when pure or nearly pure profile. In no portrait from the life, I think, does Byron appear with pen and ink, and amongst paintings of him, hardly any image shows him looking directly at the spectator, other than in the miniatures which were designed as mementoes, proxy presences in absence, for friends and lovers. Westall probably did several versions of his portrait of Byron: both reproduced here are in the National Portrait Gallery, but what I might call the sober one — probably by Westall himself and exactly his original design — is an acquisition of very recent years, while the other one has been in the Portrait Gallery since 1896, and become very widely known. It is, I think, certainly after rather than by Westall and is dated 1825; it shows, fairly repulsively, the process of apotheosis under way. As if the original were not Byronic enough, the eyes have dilated and are

Pl. 144

Pl. 145

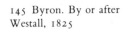

145 Byron. By or after Westall, 1825

cast heavenwards whence inspiration — but surely not for Byron — traditionally comes, while the already darkly craggy background swirls into undefined mist that seems Ossianic rather than Byronic. [54]

As counterblast to that, consider the miniature by James Holmes, painted in 1815 for Scrope Davis, with a copy significantly for Augusta Leigh. Prints of it, hand-coloured, seem also to have been produced for distribution to friends, and I reproduce one of them (in the National Portrait Gallery). This, perhaps unexpectedly, was Byron's preferred likeness of himself, at any rate for friends — as late as 1823, the year before his death, he was preferring 'that likeness to any which has been done of me by any artist whatsoever', and another time he gave the reason as Holmes's ability to take — rather an odd expression — 'such inveterate likenesses'. There seems indeed to me to be a very factual, almost stolidly prosaic air about this compared with other likenesses. Not that Holmes found him stolid, but a restless and impatient subject, who, when asked to stay still, remonstrated briskly with: 'Oh, blood and guts, do get on!' [55]

That year, 1815, was the year of his disastrous marriage, itself to last barely a year. His own personal fame increased steadily, or perhaps unsteadily — from the first cantos of *Childe Harold* to *The Corsair* and *Lara*, the formulation of the Byronic hero progressed, and when in April 1816 he went international, into an exile from which he was never to return and in a haze like a satanic halo of scandal, he was preceded into Europe by a reputation both national and international. At that moment the image in which he existed in the British mind was probably that of the then (I think) most recent portrait of him, broadcast fairly widely in an elegant stipple engraving by Meyer from the elegant original drawing by Harlow, [56] of 1815. Harlow, who died very young, was the most talented of Sir Thomas Lawrence's followers in the art of transcribing the romantic but highly controlled glamour of the Regency man of the world. Byron himself had preferred men of the world, especially the dandies of Almack's club, to men of letters, and was to become himself an integral part of the metaphysics of dandyism, developed by such as Baudelaire, Barbey d'Aurevilly, and Wilde. The founder figure of that cult had been Beau Brummell; Byron noted the essence of Brummell's image as being 'a certain exquisite propriety', and that is probably what Byron himself aimed at in everyday wear but relaxed — and this must have been deliberate — in his dress when sitting for his portrait. The Brummell image was decidedly, even glacially, formal, crystallizing the dark-clad, close-tailored, and short-cropped masculine figure into which the be-wigged and often polychrome-suited and embroidered fancy of the late eighteenth century had subsided. The 1790s saw indeed a revolution in men's appearance with the disappearance of the wig — except

Pl. 141

Pl. 146

for men of the church and of the law. The wig had been, in various forms, *de rigueur* for no less than 150 years. But while the hair went natural, though kept fairly short, the daily dress was buttoned up, and the neck in particular contained by stock or cravat. The open loose-collared Byronic shirt in his portraits may have been no more than pure vanity on Byron's own part, for at the splendour of his throat women are said to have grown pale; it became, though, an almost essential part of the Byronic myth. So Harlow has him in calculated negligence; the profile clear, pale, and sharp, the bearing arrogant and aristocratic compared with the prim, almost shy, welcome of the Holmes miniature in which the mouth borders on a smile. In the Harlow profile the downward curl of the lips is eloquent in contrast, and the delicate disarray of curls at temples and brow seems an expression of character rather than, as in the Holmes, of the attentions of the barber and a touch of Macassar. The eyes are cast down, and away.

Both images are of course, as literal translations of Byron's physique, highly mendacious. Although — as I have indicated — opinions varied, the chorus of admiration for the beauty of his person is fairly overwhelming, but what the portraits generally ignore are

146 (*left*) Byron. By H. Meyer, 1816, from a drawing by Harlow, 1815

147 (*right*) Byron. Drawing, by G. H. Harlow, 1818 (detail)

the two defects that beset him through his life. The first was that constant battle with overweight that he had to contend with from his schooldays at Harrow onwards, but especially in the last decade of his life. The second inevitably was that malformation of the left foot with which he was born, and with which he literally limped through life, ever conscious of its presence, but offsetting its handicap by concentrating on those tremendous feats of physical athleticism in sports where footwork was not so important — riding, swimming, and, not least, in bed. To Byron his lameness must have seemed the wicked fairy's curse laid on him at birth. In his legend, it has come to seem no more than an almost inevitable, almost satisfactory, confirmation that 'there is no excellent beauty that hath not some strangeness in the proportion'.

Pl. 147
Something, though, of his problem is visible in a second drawing[57] of him that Harlow made, in Venice, in 1818. The hair is long, a little limp, almost unkempt. The keen prow of the profile has softened; a sag of chin into throat is not entirely dissembled by the artist. On the other hand, the expression has shifted from the pensive disdain of the earlier drawing; it seems both more human and more humane, a touch wry perhaps. He was at this point heavily involved in amorous interludes in Venice, but also headlong into the opening cantos of *Don Juan*. The year after, Tom Moore observed that his features had lost something of 'their high romantic character' — but were more fitted for 'the expression of that arch waggish wisdom, that Epicurean play of humour'. Moore noted that maturity had even increased the striking resemblance of mouth and chin to those of the ideal beauty of the Apollo Belvedere.

Pl. 148
Five years later, Count D'Orsay, in a drawing often copied and widely known from a lithograph,[58] recorded what is probably the most faithful if unflattering impression of Byron's posture in everyday social life. In the spring of 1823, barely a year before his death, Byron saw a fair amount of that rather rum travelling *ménage à trois* — Lord and Lady Blessington and D'Orsay — who had pitched temporary camp in Genoa. D'Orsay was a prolific taker of curiously gauche but also often convincingly lively and vivid likenesses in pencil, yet was himself a great and notorious dandy. This image shows the Byronic profile, now indeed massive, sustained in some awkwardness on its body, almost too heavy for it. The dress, though, is surely as Byron dressed, the lameness of the left foot indicated, though not unkindly and barely noticeable unless you know where it is. Lady Blessington left an extensive if slightly malicious verbal portrait, diagnosing 'melancholy as the prevailing characteristic' — and yet, contradictory-wise: 'if I were to pick out the prominent defect of Lord B., I should say it was flippancy, and a total want of that natural self-possession and dignity which ought to characterise a

LORD BYRON.

148 Byron. Lithograph,
after Count d'Orsay, 1823

man of birth and education.'[59] That is perhaps no more than an unconscious recognition of Byron's versatile ability in pricking pretensions and torpedoing expectation, though it consorts not easily with the Byronic myth. More in keeping with that, at least with the sweet and sentimental side of it, are two images,[60] both made in 1822. Both, as Byron complained, swearing he would never sit again, were made on the insistence of the artists concerned: the fashionable Italian neoclassic sculptor, Bartolini, and a young American artist, W. E. West (not to be confused with Benjamin West). Byron preferred the West to the Bartolini. The West is Pl. 150 curiously bland and characterless, and was later condemned by the Countess Guiccioli as 'a caricature'. Byron's preference was perhaps largely because he was so appalled by the Bartolini. 'It exactly Pl. 149 resembles', he wrote, 'a superannuated Jesuit.' And again, 'dreadful,

149 (*left*) Byron. By L.
Bartolini, 1822

150 (*right*) Byron. By W. E.
West, 1822

Pls. 151 and 152

though my mind misgives me that it is hideously like. If it is, I cannot be long for this world.' It has blandness and tidiness in common with West's portrait, and even greater vacuousness of character plus, I think, a hint of adipose swelling. It is inadequate, but it is hard to see why Byron should have reacted quite so sharply.

It brings us, though, into the realms of the ideal sculptural representations of Byron, and is one of only two certainly made from the life. The other[61] was done earlier, from sittings in Rome in April/May 1817, at Hobhouse's request, to Thorwaldsen, the Danish sculptor, and after Canova the most celebrated of the neoclassicists. The original is now in the Royal Collection, and another version is still at John Murray's publishing house in Albemarle Street. Hobhouse had wanted it somewhat pompously laureate with 'a wreath around the brows', provoking Byron to wrath. 'I won't have my head garnished like a Christmas pie with holly — or a cod's head and fennel, or whatever the damned weed is they strew around it. I wonder you should want me to be such a mountebank.' On the other hand, according to the sculptor, he very definitely assumed a role, though a different one, when sitting, 'putting on a quite different expression from that usual to him'. Like Holmes, Thorwaldsen found his sitter restless. '"Will you not sit still?", said I — "you need not assume that look." "That is my expression", Byron said.

"Indeed?" said I, and I then represented him as I wished.' Byron, once it was over, said: 'It is not at all like me; my expression is more unhappy.' It seems, though, fairly clear that in fact he came to approve, was flattered by its existence: it was he who ordered the repeat of it for Murray in 1822. On its austere classical herm base, nobly frugal, it seems pared down to the essence and retains a vitality that answers the strength and stamina of Byron's genius if not the facets of wit and certainly not the frivolity which Lady Blessington had remarked upon.

The celebration and expansion of Byron's legacy after his death was, while international, mainly in literary terms and, when visually expressed, came by way of evocation of themes from his works rather than through posthumous celebration of his actual person.

151 and 152 Byron. By B. Thorwaldsen, 1817

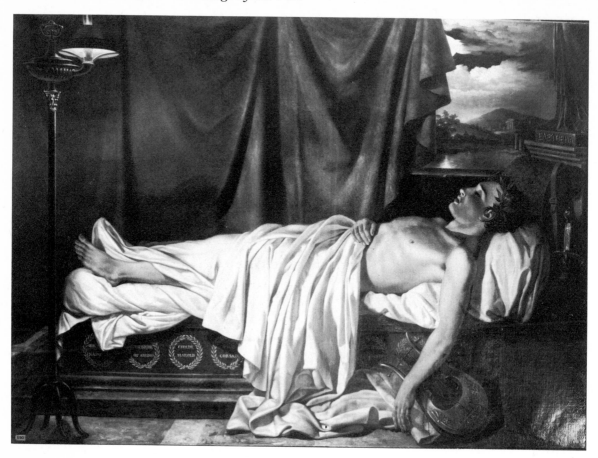

153 Byron. By J. D.
Odevaere, *c.*1826

Pl. 153

Pls. 154 and 155

The grammar and syntax of the romantic portrait in painting had
been formulated anyway well before Byron, notably in Reynolds's
works, or in specific images, like the Raeburn of Sir Walter Scott of
about 1808, or for that matter the Girodet of Chateaubriand of 1809.
Some mourning or apotheosis in painting there was. The most
curious painting, a fantasy of the body lying in state, was by a
Belgian artist called Odevaere, about 1826.[62] Willy-nilly, Byron is
now laureate, and the strings of the lyre at his bedside are broken.
Odevaere had worked with David in Paris, and this is positively
Napoleonic in feeling, recording not only the poems' titles, but the
sword against a piece of classical statuary on the right, inscribed
Liberty. It was in part as the champion of freedom that Byron, by the
manner of his death which became a martyrdom, lived on through
Europe. He was also the archetypal image of the romantic poetic
imagination. Grimm's portrait of Heine follows Westall's of Byron,
and it is Westall's image that presides, with a bust of Beethoven, over
the rapt assemblage of Hugo, Sand, Paganini, Rossini, clustered
about Liszt at the piano in Josef Dannhauser's painting, 1840.

154 (*above*) Byron. Painting,
by J. Dannhauser, 1840.
Liszt at the piano, with
Victor Hugo, George Sand,
Rossini, and Paganini, with
a bust of Beethoven and a
version of Westall's painting
of Byron

155 (*left*) Painting, by
J. Dannhauser, 1840.
Detail

156 Byron. Painting (resting
after swimming the
Bosphorus), by Sir W.
Allan, 1832

Pushkin made a drawing of Byron about 1835, and de Musset one in
1840.

In Britain, the reactions were more muted, tending to sentimental
illustration and anecdote, like Sir William Allan's reconstruction of
Byron resting up in suitably congenial circumstances after his
legendary swim across the Hellespont.[63] This was exhibited at the
Academy in 1831, but the figure of Byron conceivably goes back to
studies from the life in 1814. Still more typical of the characteristic
mid-nineteenth-century British bowdlerizing of Byron's image is an
extremely genteel water-colour of Byron on a *chaise longue* communing with the spirit of Fancy, of, I suppose, around 1830–40,
curiously reminiscent not only of Tischbein's famous portrait of
Goethe on the Campagna, but of Mme Récamier. Byron would
surely have turned in his grave, which he had by then, if with some
difficulty, found at the remote village of Hucknall Torkard. 'He was
buried like a nobleman since we could not bury him like a poet,'
recorded Hobhouse in bitterness.

Westminster Abbey and Poets' Corner had in fact been denied

Pl. 156

Pl. 157

157 Byron. Water-colour, artist unknown

him, and were to remain denied to him until 1969. After all, his morals were undeniably not all that correct. The Dean and Chapter's self-righteous rejection, however, proved in the end Cambridge's good fortune. A committee had been formed to commission a statue in 1829, and as well as Westminster, St. Paul's, the British Museum, the National Gallery, and Harrow, were all suggested as suitable sites, but none materialized. The commission seems to have been offered first to the leading British sculptor, Sir Francis Chantrey. He declined, perhaps because the money was not enough, only £1,000, but more likely because of distaste for the subject. Thorwaldsen, on the other hand, who had still the model for his bust, accepted both gladly and generously.[64] A very general suggestion of pose was supplied by the Committee ('seated not only because of the contemplative nature of poetry, but also because of the faulty foot'). Thorwaldsen then based the pose on a Hellenistic *Urania* in the Vatican that he had already used for his statue of Copernicus in 1822. Two modellos exist (in the Thorwaldsen Museum in Copenhagen), the first closer to the *Urania* pose, the second, including the symbolic broken column under Byron's foot, more or less as realized in the final marble. In that, the head, though turned, is of course based closely on Thorwaldsen's original bust from the life. On the base, Thorwaldsen added a relief, at his own cost, of the Genius of Poetry. The book in the poet's hand is *Childe Harold*. The finished statue lingered for at least five years in Customs House cellars, and only came finally to Cambridge and Trinity College Library in 1845. The

Pl. 158

158 Byron. By B. Thorwaldsen, 1830–1

writer who has most recently discussed it, H. W. Janson, thinks it a shame it should be rather hidden away in remote Cambridge. This is somewhat unfair: Cambridge not only nurtured Byron in his youth — if with some unease, bear and all — but rose in the gallery of the Senate House to applaud him when he visited in 1814, and then in 1845 welcomed him warmly back into Trinity Library. It may be that the statue is not looked at enough, but there it ought to be, in local and more than local piety, and in substance an image that delicately and happily balances neoclassic form with romantic mood.

4

The End of Fame: Tennyson and After

THE news of Byron's death, when it reached England in May 1824, was deeply felt, and that by some, like Carlyle, who were later to deplore that the poet had ever existed. In Lincolnshire, Alfred Tennyson, a boy of fourteen, went out and wrote on a rock: 'Byron is dead.' Byron was, to begin with, a marked influence on Tennyson's early work, and it chanced that Tennyson a few years later was to follow in Byron's footsteps at Cambridge and at Byron's college, Trinity. Thereafter, however, the quality of their careers diverged sharply, and though both are now reunited at Cambridge in Trinity, and both in the shape of seated statues in marble, no one would deny that they are very different. In the interval between the making of Byron's statue by Thorwaldsen around 1830, and that of Tennyson by Thornycroft in 1910, the phenomenon known as the Victorian Age had flowered, borne fruit, and, ripe for decay, was about to be axed in the holocaust of the First World War.

Amongst the innovations of the period were two that had considerable effect on portraiture in general and on the portraiture of poets in particular. The first was fundamental: the invention and rapid development of photographic techniques, from 1837 on, and the corresponding development of techniques of multiple mass reproduction of printed images. The photograph destroyed the monopoly of the artist's image: before photography, if you wanted a portrait of yourself, the only way of getting it was through the medium of an artist. Only the artist could produce an enduring memorial of your unique appearance for posterity, and it was a record which both sitter and artist could control in greater or less degree. Although professional portrait photographers discovered remarkably quickly how to disprove the axiom that the camera cannot lie, it has always retained the potentiality to produce a record of the image in front of it far more accurate, inclusive, and objective than even the most naturalistic of draughtsmen could offer — except, arguably, in the matter of colour. With film and television, the concept of even continuous portraiture has become commonplace. It is theoretically possible to record in motion the entire life, from the emergence from the womb to the consignment to the grave, of a man or woman. That prolific entrepreneur and Pop artist, Andy Warhol, has already produced hours-long fragments of such a work. If one of the results of the ubiquitous popularity of the camera has been the decay of the artist's function as recorder, as chronicler of fact, another has been a dilution of the potency of any one individual visual image. The retina of civilized man is bombarded by fabricated images remorselessly through each working day. On the other hand, especially in the case of television, the images can almost take over and real life seem at times but a shadow of reality rather than the other way round. If one finds oneself sitting opposite a television celebrity in the train, he or she may well appear — not larger than life — but smaller than television, and the same phenomenon can occur for that matter in the case of the Poet Laureate if he happens to be Sir John Betjeman. For poets, in fact, as for anyone else, the camera can multiply portraits to a degree of number and diversity at which they become difficult to range in significant order.

The other Victorian innovation that I have to single out is, in contrast to that of photography (apart from its relevance to only one sex), so literally peripheral, indeed superficial, as to seem perhaps almost frivolous. I mean the re-invention of the beard. The thought of Milton, or any of the Augustan poets — Pope especially, or Thomson, Johnson, or Gray; of, more curiously, Wordsworth or Coleridge, or Blake, or Keats, Shelley or Byron — the idea of any of them bearded is preposterous. In fact, the beard in any significant manifestation had been shaved for almost two hundred years, rather longer than what I take to be its prime obliterator, the wig, had been in fashion. Its re-sparking point seems to have been the discomfort of shaving in freezing water in the campaign conditions of the Crimea. It was around 1857 that Tennyson grew his beard, the first major British poet to do so since Shakespeare and Donne.

Before coming to the impact of those two and other innovations on the nineteenth- and twentieth-century poets, I must glance at the development of the after-image of Shakespeare. I propose to do this fairly summarily: it is not on the whole a rewarding subject at this stage. Already Charles Lamb had pronounced himself sick of the endless proliferation, the 'everlasting repetition' of images of Shakespeare 'on book-stalls, in frontispieces and on mantelpieces',[1] and that was before photography, or the steel-engraved plate, far less the half-tone block. On the other hand, we find Keats, in a letter of 10–11 May 1817 to Haydon, indicating the enduring and still-continuing function of the icon, as Pope had before him: 'I remember your saying you had notions of a good Genius presiding over you . . . Is it too daring to fancy Shakespeare this Presider?' Staying in the Isle of Wight, Keats had been attracted by an engraving of Shakespeare in his lodging-house; it was given to him by his landlady, and though now lost, it remained with him — embellished with tassels by Georgiana Keats — until his death. It is this portrait that appears on the wall in Severn's posthumous whole-

Pl. 130 length painting of Keats (see p. 119).

The variety of forms in which Shakespeare continues to appear as Presider is enormous: copies — in the mass-produced form of engravings just as in pricier paintings or casts; imaginary likenesses; porcelain or pottery bric-à-brac; even statues. I have earlier noted the heightened appreciation of the authentic original which was one facet of romanticism, and indicated that as a result, in a market where supply of the real thing was sadly lacking in both quantity and quality, demand was inevitably met by an increased supply of fakes.

The adaptation, repainting, of a genuine portrait of the time, though of someone other than Shakespeare, to look like Shakespeare — as in the case of the 'Janssen' portrait — is only one method of faking. When the Shakespeare forgery industry really got under way, in the wake of other kinds of forgeries by the Irelands — though they too had a shot at Shakespeare portraiture — it did so in some quantity, and sometimes not without some enterprise of invention, in fact some quality, though the products tend, from beneath the superior raised eyebrows of hindsight, to appear merely absurd. Two painters, in the early nineteenth century, dominated the field, the first one being Robert Holder, and the second, who had worked for a time with Holder, called Paul Henry Zincke (d. 1830). They played, mostly, variations on the theme of the Chandos painting, and I will not undermine the reader's attention by cataloguing them. Two examples will serve — though I would not swear they are by Holder/Zincke rather than by some other hand awaiting art-historical recognition. First, in the category of the

Pl. 159 absurd: the image known for obvious reasons as the Bellows portrait.[2] One can imagine someone fascinated by the lowest horrors of contemporary junk-shop/old tea-shoppe kitsch snapping it up for his collection amongst the choicer specimens of badges with images of the Bard in one form or another and available from Stratford tourist-traps; in fact, it is cherished by that admirable Johnsonian scholar, Mrs Donald F. Hyde, as a mild not-to-be-thrown-away joke in her great collection. It has indeed a venerable pedigree — made apparently by Zincke in the early nineteenth century, but acquired not so long after (already of course suitably aged by its maker) by the great French tragic actor Talma, and reverently housed by him in a specially made velvet-lined case. The second example, though

159 (*above left*) Shakespeare. The 'Bellows portrait', by C. F. Zincke

160 (*above right*) Shakespeare. The 'Ogden portrait'

161 (*left*) Shakespeare. The 'Flower portrait', by or after Droeshout

Pl. 160

probably from either Holder or Zincke's hand, has, I find, a slightly fey though not entirely negligible, even if demonstrably entirely spurious, poetry about it. It is known as the Ogden portrait: it has a primitive air, as if by some quite talented early precursor of Grandma Moses, with a delicate evocation of the Globe Theatre in the background. It is quite small, and not uncherishable — and was in fact very much cherished by the late C. K. Ogden.[3] Ogden was a scholar of inventive and original and by no means always dismissible ingenuity, most widely known as pioneering founder of 'Basic English'. He owned this portrait and was convinced of its originality. Unfortunately, his faith, as other faiths before, is undone, not only by expert opinion of art historians, but by science. Prussian blue is applied liberally in this painting, and Prussian blue was not used till the late eighteenth century.

That is, though, a grey area — not so much between the real thing and the forgery, as between the forgery, done with intent to deceive, and the pastiche which may simply be an exercise 'in the manner of', an improvisation, done for the pleasure of its maker. It may be, quite often, a genuine salute to the subject of the picture. But the closer these are to the style of the subject's own time, the more likely they are to be mistaken as the real thing. This is or may be the case with another that persists (if indeed a forgery): the painting known as the

Pl. 161

Flower portrait,[4] so close to the Droeshout print that occurs through the four Folios that it must be either the original of the print or a copy from it, or a version of a lost original from which both it and the print derive. Its pedigree is murky — an East Anglian second-hand shop, whence salvaged by Sir Desmond Flower and given by him to Stratford-upon-Avon only in 1911. It has undergone scientific analysis, by X-ray, and been shown to be overpainted on a fragment of Netherlandish religious painting. That, however, is clearly considerably earlier than the date of around 1600 that the painting on top ought to be, and so proves nothing, and indeed Stratford displays the picture with the X-ray alongside. Two things are more disturbing: first, the unanimous opinion of all who have specialized in the history of Elizabethan painting (as distinct from Elizabethan literature) that the painting is, stylistically and materially, all wrong; and secondly, that the corrugation in certain dark areas of the painting, especially the hair, can only be bitumen — a substance not used in painting till the late eighteenth century. It is, I am sure, a copy of the print; it faces the same way — that is, it is not reversed as is usual when a print is copied from a painting. I suspect it was meant to deceive — but I mention it especially as its stamina, like that of the Janssen forgery, is remarkable. It is this portrait that appears for example on the cover of Mr Anthony Burgess's spirited ex-travaganza on the subject of Shakespeare's life,[5] no doubt entirely permissibly; but to find it as frontispiece to the sober Professor Schoenbaum's otherwise admirably fastidious recent recension[6] of Shakespeare's life can somewhat startle a pedantic specialist, perhaps especially because the author in an earlier publication had dealt with the painting's claims to authenticity with his customary frank thoroughness.

The number of painted forgeries is legion, and most of them were produced during the nineteenth century. The more important – or rather, perhaps, the more likely to deceive – were investigated by one of the few reliable scholars to specialize in the iconography of Shakespeare's person: M. H. Spielmann. A series of articles by him appeared in the *Connoisseur* magazine early this century, and to those the earnest inquirer should address himself.[7] There is in fact still no comprehensive monograph on the subject, and indeed the most fully illustrated survey available at the time of writing is still Spielmann's account in the great 1911 edition of the *Encyclopaedia Britannica*. This is odd in relation to the enormous proliferation of Shakespearian literature since 1911, though perhaps odder still is the fact that it accounted for a quarter of the whole entry for Shakespeare in the *Encyclopaedia*. Spielmann never consolidated his work into a definitive volume, but his material all survives, awaiting its editor, in patient boxes stacked under Harvard Yard in Cambridge, Mass.

The most attractive kind of doubtful portrait tends to be that which is genuinely of the period, and the identification of which you cannot disprove. Unfortunately, so far no one has been able to prove either the validity of any example of this kind.

That known as the 'Grafton' portrait in the John Rylands Library   Pl. 162
at Manchester recurs fairly constantly.[8] It came to light in 1907 with no particular pedigree and no particular identification. It is, though, a perfectly genuine painting of the period, and its inscription – age 24, date 1588 – fits Shakespeare, but otherwise there are really no grounds for identifying it as Shakespeare except subjective preference. It came to prominence when Dover Wilson, while on the one hand stating the facts about the shortcomings of the evidence as to identity calmly and clearly, on the other hand, inspired by a sort of divine rage at the inadequacy of the Droeshout and the monument as portraits, raised the Grafton as, he said, 'the banner of the crusade' against them, and blazoned it as frontispiece to his *Essential Shakespeare* of 1932. There is no particular reason why it should not be Shakespeare, and it would be delightful if it were, but sadly there is no reason either, other than that the sitter is the right age, why it should be he.

More recently, Dr Hotson, in a fascinating volume full of the most recondite erudition, stated firmly that a well-known miniature by   Pl. 163
Hilliard, known in two versions, both unidentified, was in fact

162 (*left*) 'Shakespeare'. The 'Grafton portrait', 1588

163 (*right*) 'Shakespeare'. Miniature of an unknown man, by N. Hilliard, 1588

Shakespeare.[9] It depicts a most elegant blond young man, in the smartest of hats, clasping with one hand an enigmatic anonymous hand (male or female?) proffered to him from a tidy cloud above. Like the Grafton, it too is dated 1588, but this one gives no age. Professor Schoenbaum, reviewing this book, pointed out that the argument for the identification consists largely of a series of mutually reinforcing hypotheses: there is not a great deal of reason indeed why one should not believe it is Shakespeare, but though Dr Hotson has a great deal of reason at his command it does not in any way prove the subject *is* Shakespeare. Sir Roy Strong has suggested, in that the miniature has Howard connections in its provenance, that one could do worse than look for its sitter in the ranks of the Howard family. I would add another suggestion — for there is in fact one reason against Dr Hotson's identification, though he disposes of it by not mentioning it, and that is the fact that it is surely difficult to reconcile the features of the man in the miniature with those in the Stratford bust or the Droeshout engraving. But the miniature is certainly poetic in flavour, could indeed well be a poet, and if one is going to consider physical likeness, one might do worse than contemplate Edmund Spenser. Of Spenser no fully authenticated portrait exists, but the type of portrait to emerge earliest with his name — around 1719 — could perfectly well represent him.[10] In features and colouring, it is not far off those of Dr Hotson's miniature; the major drawback is the difficulty of agreeing that painter and sitter could have met in 1588. In that year, Spenser seems to have been uninterruptedly in Ireland.

164 'Byron'. Artist
unknown

Dr Hotson's interest is bright evidence of the hunger for a genuine
portrait of the genius worthy of itself. If, like Spenser indeed, one
believes platonically that 'soul is form, and doth the body make', one
is liable to have a preconceived vision of what the portrait ought to
look like. It is a very persistent urge, and it has led to strange
establishments, for example in Cambridge. Over the High Table at
Christ's College an attractive portrait of a pale young man presides as
Milton over his old College, though he cannot possibly be Milton
(on grounds of costume and age, and, some would say, likeness).[11]
Or in Trinity College, in the Hall next to the Watts of Tennyson,
there hangs a young man of spectacular romantic allure, Byronic one
would say, and so A. C. Benson, spotting it in a junk-shop at Eton,
did say and bought it and not unreluctantly gave it to Trinity, where
it still does service as Byron.[12] Everyone who inquires knows these

Pl. 164

are not Milton, not Byron; and no great harm is done, and an illusion is preserved.

In re-creations of Shakespeare, the Victorians sometimes set him, rarely successfully, in genre pictures: Shakespeare talking with Burbage or Ben Jonson. A fairly repellent one by Henry Wallis shows Shakespeare clasping Spenser warmly by the hand; but one of the more attractive ones is also by Wallis (often associated with the Pre-Raphaelites), showing Gerard Johnson carving the bust of Shakespeare for the memorial, with a sweet view of Avon and Holy Trinity church spire: a painting redolent of summertime, as if winter could never come.[13] Interesting too, this picture, in that I think it shows early record of one of the most tantalizing and recurrent of the doubtful portraits of Shakespeare. The man holding something alongside the bust seems in fact to be holding, as pattern for the sculptor, the object known as the Kesselstadt death mask, which turned up in Germany in 1847 with WS/1616 scratched on the back. It has attracted a lot of attention, is neither provable nor unprovable as Shakespeare, nor is the scratched inscription datable. It resembles

Pl. 165

165 Shakespeare. G. Johnson at work on the Stratford effigy, by H. Wallis, 1857

very little the Droeshout engraving or the Stratford monument; the last record I have of it is as advertised in a German auction room.[14]

There are also some conflated imaginary portraits. Ford Madox Brown produced one using, he claimed, elements of the three believed to be authentic, but siting these elements in what appears to be a rather florid variation of D. G. Rossetti's person.[15] I find it more repulsive by far, fine painter though Brown was, than any of the originals, seeming to show a stout alderman fiddling ridiculously with a flower. This kind of an attempt is still sometimes pursued: even by Picasso. For the quatercentenary celebrations in 1964, Sir Roland Penrose, doyen of English surrealist painters and friend of Picasso, took him photographs of the three originals. Picasso, I gather, spread them on a table, surveyed, and dashed off three drawings,[16] all much as the one here reproduced, with I suppose a certain shock value, and even thought saleable enough to impose on the covers of one of the standard paperback editions of Shakespeare's *Works*. This becomes really not much more than a gimmick:

166 (*left*) Shakespeare. By Ford Madox Brown, 1849

167 (*right*) Shakespeare. By Picasso, 1964

Pl. 167

168 Shakespeare.
Staffordshire
pottery.

Picasso's line has more life in a single millimetre than all the three
originals of Shakespeare put together, but it is Picasso's vitality and
little to do with Shakespeare. As long, though, as Shakespeare's name
is written underneath, people will look, or even if they do not look,
accept it, and use it as counter in everyday give-and-take. I have
looked before at the persistence of the Scheemakers Poets'-Corner-
statue image of Shakespeare, and its reproduction as bric-à-brac in
ceramic miniature form. About the 1850s one of its developments
reached its final mutation; in a very popular Staffordshire ornament,
the image of Shakespeare is incorporated into folk art, elevated to the

Pl. 168   aristocracy in ermine, and in features and whiskers now clearly
related to the Prince Consort.[17] This image persists as part of the
common currency of our culture, and not only of our cultural
culture. Thus Shakespeare appeared, now quite faithfully and
soberly reproduced from the statue, as witness to the stability of the
pound sterling on banknotes in the 1970s: he is at least on the £20
note. Newton, Wellington, Florence Nightingale appear on lesser
ones. But the appetite for the heroic monumental image for poets

Pl. 170   revived too: Walter Scott was allotted what reads to hindsight as a
trial run for the Albert Memorial, in Princes Street, Edinburgh, as
early as 1846. By 1872 Shakespeare appears amongst the crowded

Pl. 171   worthies on the Albert Memorial itself, though strictly subordinate,

169 Shakespeare. Version (1768) of the Westminster Abbey statue on Stratford Town Hall, and mosaic portrait on the Midland Bank, by Harris, Martin and Harris of Birmingham, 1883, beyond

170 The Walter Scott
monument, Princes Street,
Edinburgh, 1846

incidental of course to the colossal seated solo figure of Albert himself
brooding above. In Leicester Square, however, two years later, in
1874, when the Square was taken in hand for the benefit of the
citizens by a rather engaging if criminal entrepreneur, the bogus
Baron Grant, the Westminster Abbey statue was repeated full-scale.
Characteristically of the times, the inscription on the scroll is no
longer the passage from *The Tempest* about the cloud-capped towers,
but reads simply: *There is no darkness but ignorance*, from *Twelfth
Night*. Set against a backdrop of the National Dental Hospital,
flanked by cinemas, rapid-food restaurants and pubs, and censed by
the fragrance of hamburgers, he seems a little incongruous, but
maybe — *mutatis mutandis* — the original surroundings of the Globe
were not all that different in mood.

On his home ground, in Stratford, by 1900 already long
established as a shrine for pilgrims, images of the Bard were of course
rife, and now are quite dreadfully so. There are, though, amongst the
souvenir shops, the waxworks, the serious but also commercially
orientated Birthplace and the Shakespeare Institute, some attractive
renderings, even if the passing of time alone, one suspects, may
Pl. 169   justify the adjective. But the view past the Town Hall with its Poets'-

SHAKESPEARE. ILTON. GOETHE

Corner-type statue given by Garrick two hundred years ago (inscribed this time: *We shall not look upon his like again*) across to the Midland Bank, 1883, by Harris, Martin and Harris of Birmingham, has become poignantly nostalgic. In the tympanum over the door, a far echo from Byzantium, Shakespeare Pantocrator presides over the doings of banking in glimmering mosaic. The real apotheosis, a civic-monumental, triumphal set piece, was modelled by Lord Ronald Sutherland Gower and finished in 1888 — Shakespeare brooding on his high pedestal, flanked by detached statues of Lady Macbeth, Hamlet, Prince Henry, and Falstaff — all set on the approach to the town. This is the kind of monument which twenty years ago one would have been unable to lift one's eyes to contemplate but now is becoming tolerable again. The brooding seated figure is generic of its time. Scott is seated thus in Edinburgh, and the Prince Consort in Kensington Gardens. Byron was erected in 1881 similarly, though poised on a rock and with the faithful hound at his feet — a statue sponsored by Disraeli and paid for in part by the Greek Government. Once on the fringe of Hyde Park, the development of Park Lane as a major traffic route has left Byron high and dry on an island accessible only by underpass, and dwarfed by the

171 (*left*) Shakespeare. Detail from the relief (by Armstead) on the Albert Memorial, finished 1872

172 (*right*) Shakespeare. By Lord Ronald Sutherland Gower, erected 1888

Pl. 172

Pl. 170

173 Chatterton. Chatterton
receiving the Bowl of
Despair. By J. Flaxman,
c.1775−80

Hilton Hotel behind. A bland and tedious object, it is witness
anyway to a sad missed chance − the successful sculptor in the
competition was one Richard Belt; an unsuccessful one was Rodin,
whose *Thinker*, that famous object, encapsulates though naked the
preoccupations and concerns of this kind of memorial image at this
time.[18]

This was the age, however, of the peopling of the capitals of
Europe with statues, sometimes over life-size, of national heroes.
Shakespeare was even celebrated in Paris: a standing figure on the
Boulevard Haussmann, by Paul Fournier, destroyed in the holocaust
of Paris statues carried out in the Nazi occupation in 1940−4.[19]
In London he appeared also outside the City of London School
on the Victoria Embankment, 1883; a bust outside St. Mary
Aldermanbury, 1895, survives although the blitzed ruins of the
church itself have migrated to Fulton, Missouri, as a memorial to
Winston Churchill. The Poets' Fountain − featuring Shakespeare,
Chaucer, and Milton − in Park Lane vanished in 1950, but Milton
and Shakespeare, crouched in 1905 in rather too small niches, still
adorn the façade of Hammersmith Public Library. In 1912, Shakespeare joined Gower (see p. 11) in Southwark Cathedral, if in
bloodless alabaster compared with Gower's polychrome pomp,
nevertheless elegiacally prone, head propped meditative on one hand.

174 Chatterton. By Henry Wallis, 1856

Portraits of poets recumbent recur, if rarely, and generally as memorials. Chatterton, whose tragedy so poignantly set a romantic ideal, died in 1770, aged 17, by suicide by arsenic. There is no portrait from the life known; an early drawing by John Flaxman, done within a few years (about 1775—80) of the poet's death, imagines him starting up from his couch to take a 'bowl of Poison from Despair', the latter a ghastly hooded figure.[20] Flaxman also made a design, now lost, for a monument, with Chatterton 'seen dying in the arms of the Muse, while another stands weeping by'. The most famous memorial to Chatterton, however, was created much later, in 1856, when Henry Wallis, replacing Flaxman's allegorical rhetoric with exact, if exquisitely dressed, fact, using as setting the attic in Gray's Inn in which Chatterton had died, painted him dead on his bed under the window with Pre-Raphaelite precision and a sharp, cool, almost aching clarity of colour.[21] The living model who lay for that was another poet, George Meredith — then twenty-eight. Two years later, the painter eloped with his wife, even as Millais with Ruskin's wife when painting Ruskin's portrait.

For Chatterton, the artist's imagination could rove free. The process of idealization of those who left portraits, but only ones deemed unworthy by posterity, was not confined to the case of Shakespeare. Shelley's was the most striking example. Very few

Pl. 173

Pl. 174

portraits indeed were taken of him before his death in 1822. By far the best authenticated is that painted by Amelia Curran in Rome in May 1819. She – daughter of the brilliant Irish lawyer J. P. Curran – was remarkably independent for her time, living abroad and keeping herself apparently by the painting of commissioned portraits. Her painting of Shelley is now the only thing that keeps her memory alive – unfairly, as it does not compare in competence with the portrait she made at the same time of Claire Clairmont. The inference is that Shelley's was unfinished. Amelia Curran certainly was dissatisfied with it, and according to her answer to Mary Shelley had been about to burn it when Mary's letter (after Shelley's death) arrived, asking for it. Amelia states it was already scorched by the fire; that may be dramatic licence, but she may well have touched it up at that point. Mary fell on it with raptures when it arrived ('Thy picture is come, my only one! Thine those speaking eyes, that animated look; unlike ought earthly was thou ever, and art now . . .'). Otherwise, it has aroused almost as little enthusiasm as Droeshout's image of Shakespeare. Shelley's recent biographer, however, while expressing dislike of it, has drawn attention to a similarity between it and Guido Reni's portrait of La Cenci – an image that Shelley commissioned Amelia Curran to copy in Rome, with a view to using it as frontispiece for his Cenci tragedy, and there can be no doubt that emotionally Shelley identified very intensely

Pl. 175

175 (*left*) Shelley. By Amelia Curran, 1819

176 (*right*) Shelley. By George Clint after A. Curran (? and E. E. Williams)

177 Shelley. By H. Weekes (erected in Priory Church, Christchurch, Hampshire, 1854), engraved by G. Stodart

with La Cenci. A feminine, or androgynous, quality persists in the posthumous portraits of Shelley.[22]

Adjustment for posterity is visible already in the copy made of the Curran painting by George Clint, probably for the sister of E. E. Williams (who drowned with Shelley at Lerici). Clint, an Academician, was of a surer professional competence than Amelia Curran, and tidies up the hesitations, smudgings even, of the original, but prettifies, lends it a soft *sfumato*, and to an extent conventionalizes the image. In the popular images being derived by the end of the century, Shelley degenerates into a saccharine asexual presence. He was, however, accorded two full-scale monuments that amount virtually to apotheosis. The first, carved by Henry Weekes, Pl. 177 was set up by Shelley's son at the Priory Church, Christchurch, Hampshire, in 1854. The drowned poet lies as if just washed ashore, his head supported by a seated figure in whom both his wife and the Muse may be evoked, but the whole is so vividly reminiscent of a *pietà* that it must have been designed consciously so, a curious tribute to a notorious atheist. Unlike Thorwaldsen's statue of Byron, organized by a committee, that monument to Shelley was a family project, and so too was the second one, commissioned from Onslow Pls. 178 and 179 Ford in her extreme old age by Lady Shelley, widow of Shelley's son. Destined originally to mark Shelley's grave in the Protestant

178 Shelley. Monument,
marble and bronze, by
Onslow Ford. Erected 1894

Cemetery in Rome, it was denied that site and eventually, in 1894, came to rest in a special shrine in University College, Oxford, whence Shelley had been expelled in scandal eighty years earlier. Its setting is not happy, but even if it had been, the image itself would still have excited derision as it did until very recently; now it is becoming acknowledged as one of the most remarkable achievements of late Victorian sculpture. The concept is lush: the naked but immaculate body of the drowned poet in white marble held aloft on a rich, emblematic, pedestal of coloured marble and bronze. Many have noted that the prostrate figure, from behind, looks more feminine than masculine, while its most recent commentator, noting the echoes of the famous and spectacular effigy of the martyred St. Cecilia by Maderno, in the Basilica di S. Cecilia, Rome, and its affinities with Henry Wallis's vision of Chatterton, diagnosed in it 'that slight ambiguity between death and sexual lassitude which had been so much exploited during the Baroque period in the portrayal of young martyrs'.[23]

179 Shelley, by Onslow Ford

A type of memorial celebration of poets and poetry that is singularly rare in Britain is the depiction of the national pantheon in terms of Parnassus. In Europe from early on, and especially after Raphael's Parnassus in the Vatican, Apollo, the Muses, accompanied by meditative poets usually starting with Homer, had afforded a theme on which many variations were played. Lotto even produced a joke version, *Apollo asleep on Parnassus*, with the Muses going their way, and some taking flight. Mengs's ceiling in the Villa Albani was the most celebrated neoclassic variation, and Ingres, in his monumental *Apotheosis of Homer*, demonstrated in the first half of the nineteenth century that developments were still possible. Remarkably, it is in Ingres's congregation of celebrants about Homer, and not in a work by Delacroix, that Shakespeare is included — even if apparently reluctantly, somewhat squeezed in at the bottom left-hand corner.[24] In fact, Ford Madox Brown contemplated a sort of English national pantheon for his first exercise on a monumental scale, a triptych designed to represent *The Seed and Fruits of English Poetry*. Conceived in Rome in 1845, one sketch for

Pl. 180

this was finished in Hampstead in 1853. The main, central, compartment showed Chaucer reading his poems to the royal court — Chaucer (the head based on a study of Rossetti from the life), not Shakespeare, being presented here as *fons et origo* — but figures in the wings represented Shakespeare, Spenser, Milton, Pope, Byron, Burns. Goldsmith and Thomson are represented by heads in medallions, while in the cartouches the names of Campbell, Moore, Shelley, Keats, Chatterton, Kirke White, Coleridge, and Wordsworth are inscribed. However, only the central element was carried out full-scale (over 13 feet high) as Chaucer (alias Rossetti) at the Court of Edward III; the wings were omitted.[25]

Though Moore and Wordsworth were both alive when Brown first conceived his project, by 1855, when he signed his sketch, all the poets alluded to were dead. Rossetti, as noted, did appear, but in the guise of Chaucer; Tennyson, although already Laureate, did not.

The portraits of Tennyson fall into two categories, which are simply those before 1857, clean-shaved, and those from 1857 till his death in 1892, bearded.[26] The prevailing impression of Tennyson as Poet Laureate is surely that of the venerable, bearded, grand old man, but in fact when he succeeded Wordsworth as Laureate in November 1850, five months after the publication of *In Memoriam*, he was a mere forty-one, very young for the laurels — refreshingly so indeed, and with a clear and clean-cut image compatible with the

Pl. 181

ideal of the young poet. The image is delineated in a painting by Samuel Laurence of a decade earlier, widely known from lithographs.[27] Here he is thirty-one. It is one of the few portraits of which both Tennyson and his family approved. The image did not change

much until 1857, but after 1850 as Laureate he was obviously a proper subject for the monumental medium of sculpture, and this was duly provided by the one sculptor amongst the Pre-Raphaelite brethren, Thomas Woolner, rallying to the opportunity very promptly with a first medallic relief of 1850–1; with this the artist was not happy, though the definitive version of 1854–6 does not differ very much from it. This second version became very widely known from its reproduction as frontispiece to Moxon's famous illustrated edition of Tennyson's *Poems* in 1857. The aims of the revision are interesting and illuminating. In July 1856 Woolner had shown the medallion to the Brownings and, writing to Tennyson's wife, reported the Brownings as 'immensely pleased' with it: at that point Woolner had been touching it up according to Mrs Tennyson's suggestions – 'it was upon your hint', he acknowledged, 'that it "looked scornful tho' very grand". I watched his face and now have put a slight touch of sweetness that I think is of golden value.' A number of casts, in bronze and plaster, were made. Yet maybe a considerable trace of high melancholy if not scorn persists in the downward corner of the mouth. Tennyson too, like

180 The Seed and Fruits of English Poetry. By Ford Madox Brown, 1855

Pl. 182

181 (*left*) Tennyson. By S. Laurence, *c*.1840

182 (*right*) Tennyson. By T. Woolner, 1856

the heroes of his youth — Byron, Shelley, Keats — had early assignment with death: happily not his own death but that of Arthur Hallam, a proxy fate absorbed and written out in the long gestation of *In Memoriam*.

Woolner's full-scale marble bust of the same period likewise provoked approval from both the sitter and his wife. Emily Tennyson compared the 'delicate yet lofty beauty of the medallion' with 'the grandeur of the bust' — yet here the expression, though thoughtful, perhaps even somewhat melancholic, seems to be well advanced in 'sweetness' on the medallion. The original marble, dated 1857, was bought by Trinity College as early as 1859, a rare tribute to one so young amongst its living alumni; yet of course not all that young — the subject approaching fifty, but the sculpture preserving in the lineaments of its features the immortal youth of the ideal poet.[28]

Before coming to the second stage, we may glance at two images that do catch something of the man, the poet alive — that long, rather gangling physique that cohabited so engagingly with the presence of the Bard. A little pencil drawing of Tennyson aged about twenty-two — still perhaps almost an undergraduate, and the spit image of an undergraduate as he is now, has been and ever shall be, angled, entangled, in the concentration of reading; feet perhaps on the mantelpiece; also he is surely a touch myopic. It is ascribed to James Spedding, a gifted contemporary at Trinity and future editor of

Pl. 184

183 (*left*) Tennyson. By T. Woolner, 1857

184 (*below left*) Tennyson. Attributed to J. Spedding, *c*.1831

185 (*below right*) Tennyson. Reading *Maud*, by D. G. Rossetti, 1855

Bacon.[29] 'Something like Hyperion shorn of his Beams in Keats'
poem: with a pipe in his mouth', said Edward Fitzgerald of
Tennyson at that time. The pipe here is not shown, and indeed the
carcinogenic smoke-cloud of nicotine in which all through life
Tennyson brewed his poetry is an attribute that his formal portraits
shirked entirely, with one unexpected and delightful exception that I
shall come to. Another drawing, much later, is by D. G. Rossetti,
Pl. 185   noted acutely *ad vivum*: the subject again contorted, clutching a limb
as if in fear it might spontaneously get away from him, and reading
Maud (at Browning's house, 27 September 1855). One version is
inscribed by Rossetti with a line from the declamation: 'I hate the
dreadful hollow behind the little wood'. The portrait is an ironic yet
quite affectionate observation.[30]

In 1857, the razor was laid aside. Almost simultaneously, the
Victorian master-painter of great men, George Frederic Watts,
moved in upon his prey. After Tennyson's death, Watts was to write:
'It is one of the greatest glories of my life, that I was acquainted with
one of the most splendid, perhaps the most splendid, examples of
man as he might be . . .'[31] Watts was a tireless celebrator of great
men: he sought out the pre-eminent of his time; not in any sense of
social or indeed financial self-aggrandizement, but to paint portraits
as if illustrations to the anthem: 'Let us now praise famous men . . .'.
Moral grandeur was the quality he sought.[32]

Pl. 186   In his first painting of Tennyson, his grasp of that aspect is not yet
fully consummated. It is the first of seven portraits, some of which
exist in several versions and were often reproduced. Dating from
1856, it shows the beard in as it were tender springtime, and is in fact
a most seductively romantic portrait. It recalls the lyric elegance of
Van Dyck's vision of Charles I, rather than the colourful and
sonorous chords of Venetian painting at which Watts was ever more
consciously and conscientiously to aim. The actuality, as recorded
that same year, 1857, by Nathaniel Hawthorne, was not necessarily
quite as Watts's version. 'Most picturesque figure without affectation
that I ever saw; of middle size, rather slouching, dressed entirely in
black, and with nothing white about him, except the collar of his
shirt, which methought might have been clean the day before. He
had on a black wide-awake hat with a round crown and wide,
irregular brim, beneath which came down his long black hair,
looking terribly tangled; he had a long pointed beard too, a little
browner than his hair, and not so abundant as to encumber any of the
expressions of his face.' He moved, noted Hawthorne, with 'short
irregular steps – a very queer gait as if he were walking in slippers
too loose for him'.[33]

Pl. 187   With Watts's third portrait, six years later (1863–4), the translation of the poet of lyric charm into the prophet – the seer, *vates*, as

186 Tennyson. By G. F. Watts, 1856

antiquity saw its poets — is fully effected. The concentration is entirely on the head, now seen fully and solemnly frontal, brooding. The features, and the growth of the hair, are simplified: the face and nose lengthened slightly, concave and convex planes of cheeks and brows counterpoised. It is the full ideal treatment, and it is one which most of Tennyson's contemporaries would recognize as true and apt, and one which anti-Tennysonian reaction of the first half of the twentieth century would find very indigestible. The persistent romantic image of the poet was of the young poet living life and poetry as one, burned out by their joint intensity into early and spectacular death: an image containing many strains and echoes — of Sidney, of Savage's life as told by Johnson, of Chatterton — but most of all of course of that star-struck trio: Keats, Shelley, and Byron, and not at all of Wordsworth who failed the cause by growing old. It was an image that was to be reinforced by later, very differing examples — from Rimbaud to Rupert Brooke to Dylan Thomas. I remember when young disbelieving profoundly the notion that Tennyson, while pouring out his verses, lived out in his life the poetic vocation to its full. But so, for his contemporaries, he did. So Anne Thackeray said of him: 'He lived the things he said, and made us live them, for he had the power of making all men into poets for the time being.' This particular version of Watts's image seems most closely answered by Canon Rawnsley's recollection of Tennyson: a feeling of talking to 'something more than common mortality. The sound of the seer was in his voice. The art of a prophet was round about him. I had seen many great men, I had not felt one before. . . .'

Painter and poet had in common at least the intention of the grandly sublime, of simple and innocent goodness. On the aims of art they were equally in agreement, and Watts's views on the proper purpose of portraiture are said to be those incorporated in some lines of Tennyson's in *Lancelot and Elaine*, arising out of talk during the sittings for Watts's 1859 portrait of the poet:

> a painter peering on a face
> Divinely thro' all hindrance finds the man
> Behind it, and so paints him that his face,
> The shape and colour of a mind and life,
> Lives for his children, ever at its best
> And fullest . . . .

That is the quest, as old as portrait-painting itself, to portray the mind, to catch the soul, within the lineaments of the body — a task that that most reasonable and pragmatic man, Sir Joshua Reynolds, once stated firmly to be not within a painter's grasp. Yet in this melancholic almost lowering image, those eyes under the heavy

eyelids looking through and away, austere and severe against the stiff-leaf foliage of the symbolic bays or laurels and the darkening blue beyond, there is a resolute and impressive attempt to create the equivalent of 'the shape and colour of a mind and life'.

A comparison with the photograph alongside shows something of the system by which Watts hoped to achieve this — a simplification, generalization, as compared with the detailed inventory offered by the photograph. The photograph is by Julia Margaret Cameron, close friend and active pursuer of both Watts and Tennyson. The painting is of 1863/4, one of two versions; the photograph's closeness to the painting seems an instance of the undeniable influence that Watts's theory and practice of painting had on Mrs Cameron's style in photography. That may well be so, but I would not be surprised were some evidence to turn up that this particular image was inspired by the photo. The painting is the most severely general, abstracted, distanced version of Tennyson that Watts produced, and a staging of its process from its original via a still photograph might help to account for that. It is indeed, in mood as in technique, nearer to an expressionist image than a naturalistic or still less an impressionistic one.

By this time, the mid-sixties, the camera and the photograph were well established, and swifter and more reliable techniques developing rapidly. Julia Margaret Cameron's reputation, as the most

187 (*left*) Tennyson. By G. F. Watts, *c*.1863–4

188 (*right*) Tennyson. Photograph, by Julia Margaret Cameron 1863–4

Pl. 188

189 (*left*) Tennyson. The 'Dirty Monk', by Julia Margaret Cameron

190 (*right*) Tennyson. By Julia Margaret Cameron, 3 June 1869

Pls. 189 and 190

remarkable of English photographer-portraitists, still holds in spite of the much more intensive research into photographic history recently. Between 1860 and 1875, based on a house next door to Tennyson's near Freshwater in the Isle of Wight, or at Little Holland House in Kensington, she took a whole series of Tennyson. Her aesthetics were supplied by Watts, and so really were those of conventional painting, while the exploitation of the possibilities of the new medium came, when they did come, almost by mistake – soft focus, for instance. Her successes, though, are very remarkable. Of the two better-known ones of Tennyson, the one famously christened by him the Dirty Monk is not the finer – he is indeed rather like a robed prophet, rather than monk, but indubitably (Mrs Cameron would have maintained, picturesquely) unkempt. It shows one of the drawbacks of the photograph: its ability to catch not the skull beneath the skin, the essential, so much as the enlarged pores amongst it, the disturbing superficial incidents. The other, which seems to be of 1869, has all the virtues – the definition, the dignity, the veracity – of the conventional studio photograph, but avoids its posed rigor. This I find in many ways the most credible, acceptable, and humane portrait of Tennyson of all.[34]

And all there certainly were: from the time of his laureateship in 1850 till his death in 1892 there is hardly a year in which he is not recorded in one medium or another, and often a year would see several portraits of him. The potency of the ceremonial portraits –

191 Tennyson. With his
family, by Rijlander, *c.*1862

the paintings and the sculptures — seems proportionately to diminish.
Woolner's bearded bust, of 1873, though handled in a way more
severely than his earlier beardless one (in the classical treatment of the
base, for example), gives a curious slightly uneasy feeling of being
undressed, naked rather than nude, unlike the superb Hellenistic
heads of such as Homer and Euripides conceived in a comparable
mood.[35] The informality that the camera could offer, though it was
still often somewhat contrived, shows in the family group of the   Pl. 191
early 1860s. There too shows the poetic picturesque, the flowing garb
of the poet even when not overclad in great dark cloak and great
dark hat; the picturesque was imposed on the children too, as
Augustus John was to do later to his children. The last painting of
Tennyson by Watts, some twenty years on, was produced in two
versions; one was in peer's robes, in realistic acknowledgement of his
status as the first poet to be ennobled — now in Adelaide: the other
was given by the artist to Trinity, Cambridge, where it hangs in the   Pl. 192
Hall appropriately (even if slightly inappropriately in an Oxford
DCL gown). Both versions seem a little weary; both sitter and artist

192 Tennyson. By G. F.
Watts, 1890

were old men, Tennyson over eighty, Watts seventy-three. Both
spanned and all but encompassed, in certain aspects, the Victorian
age, an achievement which was to sink their reputation for many
years. Artist, sitter, and the idiom of the portrait convention itself
seem all rather exhausted, and the artificiality of the procedure shows
clearly in an illustrated paper's evocation of the sitting for this
Pl. 193   portrait, Watts peering at the ermine-swathed poet peer, who is
poised amongst an imported shrubbery of laurel in his study at
Aldworth. Watts however was not yet done. After Tennyson's
death, he rose to the challenge — and this was in 1898, when the artist
was eighty-one — of a commission from Lincoln for a colossal statue
of the town's greatest son, to stand near the cathedral. Cloaked as
ever, head bowed in meditation, a wild flower in his hand, the poet is
accompanied also by his wolfhound Karenina. (The incidence of
dogs in the heroic portraits and statuary of major British poets in the
nineteenth century is not unimpressive: Raeburn's Walter Scott (and
dogs accompanying Scott in other portraits too); the statue of Byron
by Park Lane, the dog presumably Boatswain with whom the poet
had wished to share a grave; and now Tennyson at Lincoln.) Watts
finished it in 1903, but died the year after and never saw the bronze
Pl. 195   cast from it. A photograph of him, seated, monkish, at the feet of the
plaster has survived in the Watts Gallery at Compton; some
instability in the plate over the years has swirled the sky
apocalyptically.

Trinity College's final summoning of Tennyson, the posthumous

193 Tennyson. Watts painting Tennyson

194 Tennyson. Detail from the Thornycroft statue (a pipe amongst the laurels)

statue by Hamo Thornycroft, 1910, in the ante-chapel, has, though, more vigour, and is impressive not only in its sheer weight and stature, but in dignity enlivened by some crispness of handling. And it is curiously the only formal portrait that I know that mentions Tennyson's addiction to tobacco. Low at its side you will find the regulation spray of laurel, but also, peeping out amongst the leaves, a pipe.

The true and apt figurehead for the spirit of the great lyric poet

Pl. 196

Pl. 194

195 Tennyson. Plaster for the bronze statue at Lincoln, by G. F. Watts, 1902(?)

196 Tennyson. By Sir H. Thornycroft, 1909

that Tennyson at times was, though, is surely that clear profile or bust of young manhood, and it is so that he appears not only in the substantial context of literature, at Trinity, but also by his grave in Poets' Corner, where inevitably he came to rest at Westminster. In Trinity Library, Woolner's early bust of him used to stand flanking the vista down to Thorwaldsen's superb statue of Byron: at Westminster, a version of the same bust was joined in 1969 by the inscription to Byron on a stone set in the floor, when Byron's genius was at last acknowledged there.

In 1865 Tennyson had once observed: 'Modern fame is nothing. I am up now, but I shall go down, down . . .' His deathbed in 1892 seems one of the last of the great Victorian set pieces. It was noted with grieving satisfaction at the highest level, by Queen Victoria in her journal: 'He died with his hand on his Shakespeare and the moon shining full into the window over him.' But by the time of his death the concept of immortal fame was already shrinking fast, like man in the context of Darwinian origins and expanding universes, and the belief in personal survival through eternity became ever more difficult to reconcile with scientific exploration. Interest in ideal or heroic or commemorative images of the poets waned simultaneously, and portraits became commonplace and endlessly re-duplicated; became, indeed, also in no small degree mere elements in the media of communication which Marshall McLuhan was later to claim as the message itself. Photography anyway does not accommodate the heroic, the ideal, very easily. The progress of images of Browning is a rather sad illustration.[36] One may start with

197 (*left*) Browning. By F. Talfourd, 1859

198 (*right*) Browning. By D. G. Rossetti, 1855

199 Browning. By G. F. Watts, 1866

200 Browning. Painting, by R. Lehmann, 1884

Pl. 197
Talfourd's drawing of him in the National Portrait Gallery, a little soft perhaps but undeniably soulful, in the classic pose of poetic
Pl. 198
reverie; or the slightly earlier and more convincingly sharp concentration of Rossetti's view of him, in the Fitzwilliam Museum; but the
Pl. 199
transition thence to later life is sobering. Watts's profile, in the National Portrait Gallery, is opaque, naturally averted in that pose,
Pl. 200
and unrevealing, and in R. Lehmann's late portrait he has become pure effigy. There, the conventional pose, the gloss of finish, seem to belong more properly to the bland scrutiny of the society studio photographer than to interpretative portraiture. The image would become a banker, a distinguished alderman, or perhaps, as T. S. Eliot was indeed from beginnings in a bank to become, a publisher.

Exceptions to this decay of the poet's image do occur, as with W. B. Yeats, that highly self-conscious and deliberate theorist of the mask, of course. But *the* poet, I think the only British poet of modern times, whose personal image, the image of whose person inseparable from his poetry, has impressed itself indelibly on the awareness of several generations, is Rupert Brooke.

Up to 1964 — the year of the publication of Christopher Hassall's biography of Brooke,[37] all but fifty years after his death — the famous profile of the poet could seem a pure and adequate, even more-than-adequate, image to match the poetry. F. T. Prince has in fact recently been moved to write a long poem, 'Afterword on Rupert Brooke' (1976), the starting-point of which is that image — 'what would it be without the photographs'. The original was one of a sequence taken on a rather foggy afternoon in spring in 1913 in Pimlico by an American photographer called Sherril Schell. The photographs were promoted by Francis Meynell, but the pose of the
Pl. 201
last one was suggested by Brooke — the bare-throated, bare-shouldered profile — even though at least once he referred to it as 'rather silly'. It appeared as frontispiece to *Poems 1914*, after Brooke's death on his way to the Dardanelles, subtly detached by the engraver Emery Walker to float as in an empyrean of eternity. Thence it was consolidated into the official memorial: a drawing copied from it in the National Portrait Gallery; a marble plaque likewise with the same profile, carved in relief, with the lines starting 'If I should die . . .' below, in the chapel of Rugby School; and the same image
Pl. 202
embossed on the leather binding of the *Poems* that were distributed to heaven knows how many schoolboys as prizes through the 1920s. Brooke's personal beauty — a word unusual in his time in application to a man — created a coruscation of exclamation amongst his contemporaries like the trail of a rocket. And in him, in F. T. Prince's words, there seemed to exist that rare and radiant 'identity of mould and moral substance'. To hindsight, his death and burial in the Greek Islands in his twenty-eighth year have the inevitability of a fate that

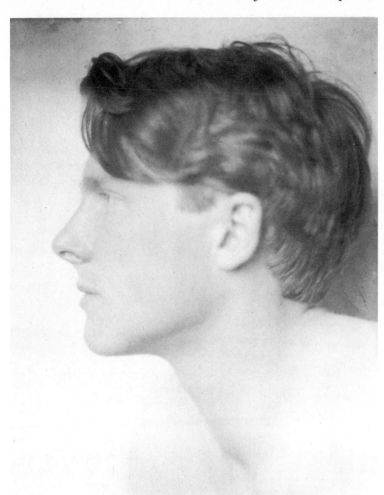

202 (*above*) The *Collected Poems*, *c.*1930

201 (*left*) Rupert Brooke. Photograph, by Sherril Schell, 1913

knew what it was up to: as Henry James observed at once when he heard the news – 'Of course, of course.'

The purity of the profile provoked the inevitable reaction, inseparable as it is from the heroics of the war sonnets. Only perhaps after Hassall's biography, deepening and shadowing, perplexing and humanizing the ideal image, did the attention of younger readers come back to the poetry. Meanwhile, that had receded before the disillusion of the second wave of First War poets, like Sassoon and Wilfred Owen. Of Sassoon, shy and elusive, intensely private, there is no widely known image. That in the Fitzwilliam Museum was painted in the midst of his wartime revolt, in 1917, by Glyn Philpot.[38] As Sassoon records, no doubt with some irony, it is both a romantic and an externalized image: he called it in fact 'an ideal "posterity portrait" for a writer', and though competent, it adds little to that convention. The finest poet of them all, Owen, is

Pl. 203

203 (*left*) Siegfried Sassoon.
By Glyn Philpot, 1917

204 (*right*) Wilfred Owen.
Photograph, 1916

virtually invisible behind the routine photographs of the commercial studios. Just so, uniform checked as if for inspection, hair and moustache precisely trim, thousands of young officers were photographed before departure for the Western Front, and in thousand upon thousand cases, as Owen's, for death. But Owen's photographs seem to have little bearing on his poetry.

With Yeats of course the situation both is very different, and ought to be, in response to his view of the function of what he called the mask — 'style, personality — deliberately adopted and therefore a mask'.[39] Life and work were projected in a series of styles, to which ideally no doubt he would have matched a changing series of faces. There are essentially perhaps three phases: the early one, up to his early or mid-thirties, to around 1900, dominated by the series of portraits of him by his father, J. B. Yeats — not only a professional portrait painter of great sensitivity but a marvellously articulate critic and wit. With his son, though, he was over-sensitive: and the conception is over-poetic, frail, almost fey, almost weak.[40] The poet Yeats himself, unlike Byron, was brought to approve of the portrait frontispiece very early. Gerard Manley Hopkins was a bit startled when father Yeats thrust his son's first publication on him in 1886: it had a portrait frontispiece already. In the decade between 1900 and

Pl. 205

205 W. B. Yeats. Water-colour, by J. B. Yeats, 1898

206 (*far left*) Yeats. By Max Beerbohm: Mr W. B. Yeats presenting Mr George Moore to the Queen of the Fairies, for *The Poets' Corner*, 1904

207 (*left*) Yeats. By Augustus John, 1907(?)

208 Yeats. Etching, by
Augustus John, 1907

1910 Yeats's attention was focused on the problem of finding the
right image, especially in relation to the collected *Poems* of 1908.

The portraits that resulted were varied, and Yeats's reactions to
them mixed and inconsistent, partly owing perhaps to Lady
Gregory's unfavourable reaction to all of them. As Michael Holroyd
has observed, it was all but impossible for any artist to catch Yeats as
Lady Gregory saw him and wanted him. Yeats once thought of
reproducing the variations in his *Works* with an essay describing
them 'as all the different personages that I have dreamt of being but
never had the time for'.

It is Augustus John's that has survived best.[41] John was summoned
Pl. 206   to Coole in 1907, stayed, and made a number of studies. Some of
these updated, but kindly, the image that had been burlesqued by
Pl. 207   Max Beerbohm in his *The Poet's Corner* of 1904: 'Yeats introducing
George Moore to the Queen of the Fairies'. John remembered Yeats

209 Yeats. By Augustus
John, 1907

'slightly bowed and with his air of abstraction, walking in the
garden . . . with Augusta Gregory, discussing literary matters'. And
again, 'with his lank forelock falling over his russet brow, his myopic
eyes and hieratic gestures, he was every inch a twilight poet.'

The end-product was to be an etching for reproduction in the
Works. First sight of the oil studies made Yeats a bit nervous, but he   Pl. 209
consoled himself with the thought that John's great strength was as
an etcher, only to be dismayed when the etching arrived, while Lady   Pl. 208
Gregory was appalled. Yeats saw himself in the etching as 'a sheer
tinker, drunken, unpleasant and disreputable, but full of wisdom, a
melancholy English Bohemian, capable of anything, except living
joyously on the surface'. John himself was not unduly put out, noting
that 'Painting Yeats is becoming quite a habit. He has a natural and
sentimental prejudice in favour of the W. B. Yeats he and other

210 Yeats. Photograph, by
A. L. Coburn, 1908

people have been accustomed to see and imagine for so many years. . . . I cannot see in him any definite resemblance to the youthful Shelley in a lace collar.' The etching was not used in the 1908 edition, but it was in several later ones, and Yeats himself came in the end to appreciate it, growing perhaps indeed, if briefly, more like it, as sitters notoriously do to really successful portraits of themselves. Having at first seen in it 'an unshaven, drunken bartender', he came to feel 'John had found something that he liked in me, something closer than character, and by that very transformation made it visible. He found Anglo-Irish solitude, a solitude I have made for myself, an outlawed solitude.' It is indeed a forceful and haunting image, while its roots in the reality of the physical presence are evident in comparison with one or two photographs of the time, notably those by Alvin Langdon Coburn.[42] One that is easily reconciled with John's version was actually used in the *Poems, Second Series*, of 1909. But also used about that time was an odd

Pl. 210

conventional three-quarter length by Shannon, showing him elegantly pale by a table on which reposes a spray of laurels.[43] The most
favoured of all, for the time being, seemed to be Sargent's charcoal
drawing, which does come perhaps undesirably close to the generic
concept of the poet as a youthful Shelley, if not lace-collared,
nevertheless formidably falling-locked.[44] The mask that fitted for
the time was surely that provided by John, though not recognized as
such by Yeats till later.

Still later the mask would change again, in key with that
formidable shift of style of Yeats's poetry in his old age. There is no
adequate image. Photographs indicate something of the externals,
the self-proclaimed 'sixty-year-old smiling public man'. He had
changed indeed: Max Beerbohm, who liked to trap his characters
and keep them trapped, noted regretfully as early as 1914 that he
found it difficult to draw Yeats any more, that he seemed to have
become subtly less like himself.[45] More true to himself, most critics
would claim now, but in his person elusive. John painted him again,
in 1930. John found him much changed too: 'now a silver-haired old
man, much mellowed and humanised'. Something perhaps of that is
seen in the painting, but the rather limply manic hair, given off
almost like ectoplasm, seems a somewhat forced attempt at indication of poetic character and John's powers by then were already
diluted from his intense focus of 1908. The image I personally
treasure is that of Yeats at the microphone, broadcasting, in 1937:[46]

211 (*left*) Yeats. Painting, by
Charles Shannon, 1908(?)

212 (*right*) Yeats. Drawing,
by J. S. Sargent, 1908

Pl. 213

190

213 (*right*) Yeats. By
Augustus John, 1930

214 (*below*) Yeats.
Photograph, Yeats broad-
casting, 1937

here there is something more sharply manic, properly so, but also
great strength, in the frailty of old age. But there is no image, no
mask of this time to which one can turn with much illumination
when reading the late *Poems*.

The portraits of Yeats, prolific though they are, have not really
adhered to the growth of his reputation: they are not part of the
legend as are Rupert Brooke's. Nor has any recent poet survived
really in his person, compelling itself on the popular imagination –
none of the Second War poets, and not even Dylan Thomas, burned
out though he was in relative youth assailing in intoxication the
endless platforms of American culture. A great part of the reason lies
not only in that meaningless proliferation of images available that I
mentioned earlier, but in the decay of the art of portraiture through
the first half of the twentieth century, when almost all artists of any
originality were uninterested in it, pursuing rather Roger Fry's
formal values in painting to the brink of abstraction and beyond.

T. S. Eliot is a case in point. There is little of him other than
photographs. Wyndham Lewis's portrait of 1938, though apparently odd enough at the time to cause its rejection by the
Academy and huge public uproar, seems now very conventional,
inexpressive in characterization, though a tantalizing encapsulation
of publisher/critic/poet in the armour uniform of invisible ordinary
man.[47] In context with Wyndham Lewis's work it is more
informative about that than it is, in context with Eliot's work, about
his poetry. Patrick Heron's view, extrapolated from three realistic
studies from the life in 1948, is a more enterprising attempt to

Pl. 214

215 (*left*) Eliot. Photograph, 1926

216 (*centre*) T. S. Eliot. By Wyndham Lewis, 1938

217 (*right*) Eliot. By Patrick Heron, 1948

produce an equivalent of the poetic style, its ambiguities, its transparencies, and its obscurities.[48] But it is still far from matching the poetic achievement, and again in the end asserts the painter's predominance over his subject-matter rather than that mysterious compromise kindling between painter and sitter that could happen in the great portraits of the past.

Eliot, advocate of 'extinction of personality', was famous for his rejection of the picturesque poet's garb. Sober-suited. It is difficult to credit a recent biographer who reports him about the time of his first marriage, in 1915, as at times like 'a Harvardian Rupert Brooke — with a Gioconda smile, dimples, and a graceful neck'.[49] It is even more of a shock to discover him described as late as 1922 with a dusting of green powder on his cheeks ('pale, but distinctly green, the colour of a forced lily-of-the-valley') — an impression confirmed *con var.* in Virginia Woolf's Diary (12 March 1922): 'Clive [Bell] . . . says he used violet powder to make him look cadaverous.' Some photos do show something, if not quite all that, then agreeably almost *louche*, not Prufrock exactly, but the author of Sweeney Todd perhaps about to move into partnership with Kurt Weill.

Pl. 215

One poet who was certainly not always sober-suited was Edith Sitwell. It is refreshing at last to bring a female poet on stage. The Muse herself is feminine, and Sappho has a long line of descendants. Statues of Sappho are recorded very early though no contemporary ones survive: she figures, often bearing a lyre, on Greek vases, and Mytilene struck coins bearing her image.[50] Those who followed in her poetic footsteps in England were not thus celebrated, but then none of them approached her renown. Ladies generally did not write poetry, seriously. Only in the eighteenth century do woman poets begin to be recorded in their poetic character, but even so the record is disappointing. Anna Seward, the Swan of Lichfield, for instance, whom we have glimpsed in relation to Brooke Boothby, was painted by Romney in 1786; she has the attributes but is very self-consciously posed: one hand to cheek, eyes cast upwards, scroll in the other hand, garland of laurel leaves, ink-pot, quill, and papers on a table at her side.[51]

In the nineteenth century very remarkable women poets were emerging, and becoming known to a wide public. Elizabeth Barrett Browning (who was surely the first woman to be at least rumoured as next Poet Laureate — after Wordsworth's death in 1850, when the honour went in fact to Tennyson) and Christina Rossetti are the most celebrated. Elizabeth Barrett Browning's portraits (surprisingly few) dwell on her femininity over-exclusively and somewhat sentimentally.[52] Christina Rossetti on the other hand had the bonus of a fine artist as brother and recorder of her appearance. Even so, the drawings — over a dozen — that he made of her were family records,

CHRISTINA ROSSETTI
del. SEPTEMBER 1866

218 Christina Rossetti. By D. G. Rossetti, 1866

Pl. 218

and mostly not published.[53] Though she is probably best known (from the chance of its having been in the National Portrait Gallery since 1895, the year of her death) by the severe, somewhat Dantesque, near-profile aligned with that of her mother, the most beautiful evocation is surely her brother's drawing of 1866, showing her poised rapt in contemplation, gazing away from the open book in front of her, that has always remained a family possession. It suggests, scarcely less than in the case of Rupert Brooke, an 'identity of mould and moral substance', and is as convincing a suggestion of a poet in thrall to the sound of unseen voices as any known to me, although prosaically one can classify it as yet another variant on the archetypal poetic head-on-hand pose.

It is, though, only with Edith Sitwell that the female poet claims explicitly her rightful place in the critical and public limelight.[54] Maybe she exaggerated: F. R. Leavis's censorious comment is not easily forgotten – 'The Sitwells belong to the history of publicity, rather than of poetry.'[55] The two categories are, however, by no means exclusive, as Alexander Pope had been the first to demonstrate, especially by propagation of the poet's fame through the medium of portraiture. For Edith Sitwell, Pope was the great forerunner, and she identified strongly with him in her emotionally highly-charged biographical rhapsody. The portrait of him in the

219 (*left*) Edith Sitwell. By A. Guevara, 1919

220 (*right*) Edith Sitwell. By Wyndham Lewis, 1925–35

EDITH SITWELL

221 Edith Sitwell. By Wyndham Lewis, 1921

National Portrait Gallery attributed to Richardson (Pl. 80) moved her 'almost to tears'.[56] Further, she projected her personality as spectacle in daily life as Pope had not, through extravagance of dress and even, as famously in the various performances of *Façade*, on stage. Her status as poet, and especially as female poet, was a continual obsession, her official honours accepted proudly and her titles worn like medals. There was her doctorate, and then her accolade as Dame: 'Until now writing poetry was supposed in my case' (and 'in my case' I think she included the consignment to obscurity of the whole race of women poets who had preceded her) 'to be on a level with *knitting*.'[57]

Her friendships with artists, sometimes stormy and in one case apparently the love affair of her life (with Pavel Tchelitchew), bore a rich harvest of portraits. John Pearson's claim, that 'her interest in painting was more or less confined to portraits of herself', seems scarcely overstated.[58] Two, both well known, having been for many years in the Tate Gallery, are constantly cited as outstanding examples of twentieth-century English portraiture. The earlier, by Alvaro Guevara, that rather dizzy whole-length seen as if from above in steeply-tilted perspective, was shown in 1919 as 'The Editor of *Wheels*'.[59] It is an image of compact, self-contained composure. Wyndham Lewis's painting, begun in 1925, 'finished' only in 1935, was the outcome of (according to the subject's own – possibly exaggerated – account) sitting six days a week over ten months:[60]

Pl. 219

222 (*left*) Edith Sitwell. Photograph, by Cecil Beaton (for *The Book of Beauty*, 1930)

223 (*right*) Edith Sitwell. By Rex Whistler, design for dust-jacket of her biography of Pope

'in the end his manner became so threatening that I ceased to pose for him, and his portrait of me has, consequently, no hands.' Friendship gave way to lifelong vendetta, but the painting has a brittle brilliance, fragmented yet hieratic, that goes well with her early poetry, which delighted me when I was a boy, even if, on coming unawares across her literary polemic, I was startled by the virulence of her invective and I was never able to come to terms with the rhetoric of her later post-Blitz, post-Bomb work. Perhaps one or two of Lewis's drawings are the best, loaded and dangerous as some antique armour designed for parade but no less effective for tournament and battle. The long sequence of photographs by Cecil Beaton summons up an entirely different image: Beaton acknowledged that for him she was 'in all her guises' 'an outstandingly beautiful object, aesthetically flawless'. In his *Book of Beauty*, opposite a passage of the purplest prose, he reproduces the poet simulating her own prostrate effigy.[61] Yet the most charming evocation of her in her poetic role that I know is a design that Rex Whistler made for the dust-jacket of her *Alexander Pope* — an elegant pastiche of Gainsborough's Garrick communing with the bust of Shakespeare.[62]

Pl. 220

Pl. 221

Pl. 222

Pl. 223

The younger poets of the thirties — Audens, Spenders, MacNeices — all seemed almost too ordinary, tending to appear in amateur snapshots wearing mackintoshes in rough weather on Hampstead Heath. The need too for presiding icons — for a presider at all, as Keats had wanted a portrait of Shakespeare — vanished, with all the traditional trappings of the author: there are not even the servants any more to dust the icon of a presider. Auden wrote a brief irreverent obituary on that mode: 'The day of the Master's study with its vast mahogany desk . . . its busts of Daunty, Gouty and Shopkeeper . . . is over for ever. From now on the poet will be lucky if he can have the living room to himself for a few hours or a corner of the kitchen table on which to keep his papers . . .'[63] In 1976, in the course of the poet Vernon Scannell's Arts-Council-sponsored sojourn in the Oxfordshire village of Berinsfield as resident poet — a disastrous stint — the television interviewer asked a typical Berinsfield native if Mr Scannell looked like a poet. 'Oh, no,' she said. Poets, she said, 'are dirty, and they've got beards and scruffy clothes.'[64] Like, though perhaps not all that like, Mrs Cameron's photographs of Tennyson as the Dirty Monk.

The position of the poet in the social hierarchy is indeed now obscure, almost non-existent as the occupation of the full-time professional poet has become uneconomic, merely a passport to poverty. In company with that goes a tendency, since the war, of many poets to distance their persons from their work: for one school of critics the work itself is the sole object of attention, any consideration of the poet's biography in relation to the work being a frivolous irrelevance. The only poet of any substance whose person is recognizable to other than specialists is the Poet Laureate, Sir John Betjeman. But the admirable Betjeman has achieved that through the medium of television and with the aid of extremely skilful histrionic techniques that owe not a little to the tradition of the music-hall. Apart from him, television, now the dominant medium of communication for the general culture of any nation, has yet to be conquered by serious poetry.

Amongst the dead poets, the only personal image that hovers, instantly recognizable, in the public awareness is probably that of Shakespeare, that ever-developing constant to which I have referred back throughout. He is still with us; I have reproduced examples enough of recent reformulation and I will not labour the point with newspaper reproductions of Shakespeare opening the new super-market, or the do-it-yourself cut-out cardboard bust on one side of the jumbo pack of Kellogg's Cornflakes. Their relevance to Shakespeare's work is dubious and rather painful. I would instead close with a look at a poet I have not so far mentioned: Thomas Hardy. Very far from the ideal romantic poet falling like Icarus in his prime: shrinking, rather, physically into his extreme old age. At first glance he was not generally impressive, as Rupert Brooke found: 'Incredibly shrivelled and ordinary and made faintly pessimistic remarks about the toast.' Shy and yet not shy, he retained a kernel of secrecy and privacy not divulged in ordinary intercourse.

In Somerset Maugham's *Cakes and Ale*, his best book perhaps, the two protagonists, Alroy Kear and Edward Driffield, are agreed to be Hugh Walpole and Thomas Hardy, lightly veiled. At the end, the narrator is riffling through old photographs of the now dead writer character, Driffield, who is Hardy, groping for the essence of the reality, of the unique individual, and comes to the conclusion that that is a 'wraith', 'a wraith that went a silent way unseen between the writer of his books and the man who led his life, and smiled with ironical detachment at the two puppets that the world took for Edward Driffield'.

Hardy said much the same to Shakespeare in a lovely poem, written in 1916 on the tercentenary of Shakespeare's death:

> Bright baffling Soul, least capturable of themes,
> Thou, who display'dst a life of commonplace,
> Leaving no intimate work or personal trace
> Of high design outside the artistry
> > of thy penned dreams,
> Still shalt remain at heart unread eternally . . .

In fact the portrait-takers pursued Hardy briskly, and generally found him baffling too, and Kennington's memorial statue of that rather misleadingly dear old man surprised at finding himself in stone

Pl. 224

224 Thomas Hardy. By Eric Kennington, 1930–1

knickerbockers seated slightly above the common level of Dorchester is probably the latest and last statue of a poet to be erected on these shores.[65] There is, though, one admirable shot at Hardy, preserved in the Fitzwilliam Museum at Cambridge. It is by Augustus John, who was provoked to his best, as not uncommonly, by the literary man. This is Hardy in 1923, and Hardy was pleased, paying John one of the most warming compliments that a sitter can pay to his artist: 'I don't know whether it's like me — but it's what I feel like.' The initial study, the drawing, without the bookshelved setting that Auden was to indicate as obsolete, is even finer, exhilarating.[66]

Yet it is all a vanity really; I am grateful to those readers who have borne with me in its pursuit thus far, and will leave them to more proper concerns than the emptied portraits of persons, or the essential wraiths that elude them, back to Ben Jonson's admonition in the closing couplet of his verses that accompany that both best-known, and worst, of contemporary portraits of Shakespeare, Droeshout's engraving:

Reader, looke
Not on his Picture, but his Booke.

225 Hardy. By Augustus John, 1923

Notes

References are given in full, apart from the following abbreviations:

Blanshard, *Wordsworth* — Frances Blanshard, *Portraits of Wordsworth* (London, 1959)

Hind, *Engraving* — A. M. Hind, *Engraving in England in the Sixteenth and Seventeenth Centuries*, 3 vols. (Cambridge, 1952–64; vol. III was compiled by M. Corbett and M. Norton)

Keynes, *Blake* — Geoffrey Keynes, *The Complete Portraiture of William Blake* (London, 1977)

Ormond — R. Ormond, *Early Victorian Portraits* (London, 1973), 2 vols.

Parson, *Keats* — D. Parson, *Portraits of Keats* (Cleveland and New York, 1956)

Piper, *Catalogue* — D. Piper, *Catalogue of the Seventeenth Century Portraits in the National Portrait Gallery* (Cambridge, 1963)

Piper, *Literary Portraits* — D. Piper, 'The Development of the British Literary Portrait up to Samuel Johnson' in *Proceedings of the British Academy*, LIV, pp. 51–72

Piper, *Shakespeare* — D. Piper, *O Sweet Mr Shakespeare I'll have his Picture* (National Portrait Gallery, London, 1964)

Spielmann, *Conn.* — M. H. Spielmann, articles on doubtful Shakespeare portraits in the *Connoisseur Magazine*:
1. Vol. XXII (1908), p. 73: 'Belmont Hall' portrait
2. Vols. XXIV (1909), p. 230; XXVI (1910), p. 105; XXVII (1910), p. 151; XXXII (1912), p. 18: 'Janssen or Somerset' portrait
3. Vol. XXIII (1909), p. 97: 'Grafton and Sanders portraits'
4. Vol. XXI (1908), pp. 167, 248: 'The Marriage Picture'

Strong, *Icon* — R. Strong, *The English Icon* (London, 1969)

Strong, *Tudor etc.* — R. Strong, *Tudor and Jacobean Portraits*, 2 vols. (London, 1969)

V & A, *Byron* — Anthony Burton and John Murdoch, *Byron, Catalogue of the Byron Exhibition*, Victoria and Albert Museum, London, 1974

Wellek and Ribeiro	*Evidence in Literary Scholarship* (Essays in memory of J. M. Osborn), ed. R. Wellek and A. Ribeiro (Oxford, 1979)
Whinney	M. Whinney, *Sculpture in Britain 1530—1830* (Harmondsworth, 1964)
Wimsatt	W. K. Wimsatt, *The Portraits of Alexander Pope* (New Haven and London, 1965)
Yeats, 1961	W. B. Yeats: *Images of a Poet*, Exhibition Catalogue (Manchester and Dublin, 1961), ed. D. J. Gordon and Ian Fletcher

CHAPTER I

1. G. M. A. Richter, *The Portraits of the Greeks*, 3 vols. (London, 1965), is the fullest account, with exhaustive illustrations, of Greek portraiture, including that of the poets. The statue at Copenhagen is reasonably if not definitively identified as Anacreon; generally described as a Roman copy of a Greek original of *c.*440 BC, perhaps by Phidias. It relates conceivably to the statue set up on the Acropolis, though the subject's attitude does not necessarily suggest drunkenness (Richter, I, pp. 75—8; No. 5, figs. 278, 279, 283).

2. R. P. Hinks, *Greek and Roman Portrait Sculpture* (1935), 1976 edn., p. 17, fig. 5.

3. Rembrandt's bust of Homer appears in his famous *Aristotle*, 1653 (Metropolitan Museum, New York). See J. S. Held, *Rembrandt's Aristotle* (Princeton, 1969), pp. 17—18, 21—8.

4. *Poets at Work*, ed. C. D. Abbott (New York, 1948), p. 177.

5. K. Schefold, *Die Bildnisse der antiken Dichter, Redner und Denker* (Basel, 1943), p. 170, suggests that while the face is clearly damaged (from the nose to the right-hand corner of the mouth), it 'muss ein zeitgenössisches Bild des Dichters aus dem End seines Lebens recht getreu wiedergegeben habe'. That is however entirely speculative. Schefold suggests a date as late as about AD 300 for the mosaic; it was found at Susa, the ancient Hadrumetum, near Carthage, and is now in the Museum of the Bardo, Tunis. The attendant Muses are Melpomene and Clio. David L. Thompson, 'Painted Portraiture at Pompeii' (in *Pompeii and the Vesuvian Landscape*, Smithsonian Institution, Washington DC, 1979), touches illuminatingly, with documentation, on the general problem of Roman painted portraiture.

6. E. Hodnett, *English Woodcuts 1480—1535* (Oxford, 1935), No. 2287, fig. 229, reproduces the version that appeared (without the identification) in J. Rastell's publication of Skelton's *Agaynste a comely Coystrowne*. That is not dated but Hodnett suggests that *Dyvers Balettys*, in which the cut also appears, is of 1525—30.

7. Since going to press, a major reappraisal of Chaucer's early portraiture has appeared by J. Seymour, *Burlington Magazine*, cxxiv (1982), pp. 618—23.

8. For Richard II's portraiture, see the summary in Strong, *Tudor etc.*, I, pp. 260—2.

9. BL Add. MS 5141: rep. Strong, *Tudor etc.*, II, pl. 84.

10. National Portrait Gallery, London, No. 532. See Strong, *Tudor etc.* Belonged to Sir Hans Sloane and very possibly a very early piece of library furniture, probably late 16th century.

11. Royal Commission on Historical Monuments, *London*, Vol. V: *East London* (1930), p. 65, as of 1408 (the year of Gower's death). The date of erection seems in fact obscure. It has been moved at least twice. The books are each

titled: *Vox Clamantis* (Latin); *Speculum meditantis* (French); *Confessio Amantis* (English).

12. For Wyatt's portraiture, see Strong, *Tudor etc.*, I, pp. 338–9; II, pls. 670–3. Holbein's original of the near-profile type is missing; derivatives show the sitter dressed either normally or *all'antica*, with a loose drapery about throat and shoulders, hinting at a toga. This type was first published in a woodcut in Leland's *Noenia*, 1548. The *all'antica* fashion recurs at the end of the century, notably in miniatures by Isaac Oliver, not necessarily of poets, though in larger portraits both Herbert of Cherbury and John Donne seem to reflect it. For Surrey's portraits, see Strong, *Tudor etc.*, I, pp. 307–8.

13. *The Autobiography of Thomas Whythorne*, ed. J. M. Osborn (Oxford, 1961).

14. Strong, *Tudor etc.*, I, pp. 276–86, includes a full account of the Chandos painting of Shakespeare, and its provenance, with a summary account of the general iconography and (very select) bibliography. While this book was in the press, Mary Edmond has published (*Burlington Magazine*, CXXIV, 1982, 146–9) a very plausible suggestion that the artist of the Chandos portrait was one John Taylor (fl. before 1626–*c*.1650), a prominent member of the Painter-Stainers Company in London. The fullest and best technical accounts of the Droeshout engraving and the Stratford bust are respectively in Hind, *Engraving*, II, pp. 354–9, pls. 221–3, and P. B. Chatwin, 'The later Monumental Effigies of the County of Warwick', in *Trans. of the Birmingham Archaeological Society*, LVII (1933), 122–6. Since the latter publication, the bust was removed from its niche by vandals, in 1973, but was only superficially damaged. When it was replaced, the two mourning cherubs at the top were set the wrong way round, but this has now been corrected.

15. Hind, *Engraving*, II, p. 318, pl. 197. Frontispiece to Chapman's *Whole Works of Homer, etc.*, 1616.

16. For the Johnson or Janssen family of sculptors, see K. A. Esdaile: *English Monumental Sculpture since the Renaissance* (1927), pp. 117–21; 'Some Fellow Citizens of Shakespeare in Southwark', in *Essays and Studies* (English Assocn.), NS V (1952), 26–31.

17. H. Wivell, *An Historical Account of the Monumental Bust of William Shakespeare* (1827), p. 22, quoting the Stratford vicar of the time.

18. Quoted by R. Freeman, *English Emblem Books* (1948), p. 15.

19. See pp. 151–2.

20. Rijksmuseum, Amsterdam Holland. Reproduced by E. Auerbach, *Nicholas Hilliard* (1961), pl. 94; a version, head and shoulders only, is in the Fitzwilliam Museum, Cambridge (Auerbach, op. cit., pl. 95). The melancholic strain in late Elizabethan and Jacobean portraiture is fully discussed in R. Strong, *Icon*, pp. 352–3 (an article reprinted from *Apollo*, 1964). The melancholia of the 'malcontents' was not confined to poets, but they were one of the classes of men whom it most became. Cf. R. Burton in the *Anatomy of Melancholy* (ed. A. R. Shillito, 1926,.I, p. 461): 'melancholy men of all others are most witty, causeth many times divine ravishment, and a kind of enthusiasmus . . . which stirreth them up to be excellent Philosophers, Poets, Prophets, etc.'

21. Auerbach, op. cit., pl. 224.

22. A summary outline of Herbert's portraiture in Piper, *Catalogue*, pp. 164–5.

23. Donne's portraits are described in Sir Geoffrey Keynes, *Bibliography of the Works of John Donne* (Cambridge, 2nd edn. 1932), pp. 138–84; Strong, *Tudor etc.*, I, pp. 65–6; II, pls. 118–23.

24. J. Bryson, 'Lost Portrait of Donne', in *The Times*, 13 Oct. 1959. The black floppy hat no less than the black cloak was integral to the typical malcontent's costume. Cf. the doggerel verses on the melancholic dramatist John Ford:

'Deep in a dump Jack Ford alone was got, / With folded arms and melancholy hat' (from the 'Time-Poets', *Choice Drollery*, 1656).

25. Dame Helen Gardner, 'Dean Donne's Monument in St. Paul's', in Wellek and Ribeiro, pp. 29–44.

26. A summary account of Milton's portraiture is in Piper, *Catalogue*, pp. 235–8 and (the 'Onslow' portrait) 394–7, with earlier bibliography.

27. Leo Miller, *Milton's Portraits* (special issue of the *Milton Quarterly*, Ohio University, 1974); reviewed by D. Piper, *Notes and Queries*, Feb. 1979, 70–2.

28. The Faithorne portrait, with particular relevance to the Princeton pastel, is discussed at length in J. R. Martin, *The Portrait of John Milton at Princeton* (Princeton, 1961).

29. Dugdale Family collection, Merevale Hall (courtesy of the late Sir William Dugdale). I am uncertain whether this is by Dugdale himself from his original notation on the spot, or copied by an amanuensis from it.

30. Hind, *Engraving*, III, p. 129, pl. 71.

31. In the Frick Collection, New York. *The Frick Collection*, Vol. I (New York, 1968), pp. 194–7; see also T. Clayton, 'An Historical Study of the Portraits of Sir John Suckling', *Journal of the Warburg and Courtauld Institutes*, XXIII (1960), 109; M. Rogers, in *Burlington Magazine*, CXX (1978), 741–5.

32. Engraved in mezzotint (as Shakespeare) by J. Simon, probably in the 1730s; the antiquary George Vertue in 1731 first recorded the story of an actor sitting as Shakespeare, but to Lely rather than Soest ('Notebooks', *Walpole Society*, XXIV (1936), 13–14).

33. D. Piper, 'The Chesterfield House Library Portraits', in Wellek and Ribeiro, pp. 179–96.

CHAPTER 2

1. The most recent account of Kneller's Kit-cat Club portraits, in the National Portrait Gallery, is J. D. Stewart's in *Sir Godfrey Kneller* (exhibition catalogue) (London, 1971), Appendix, pp. i–xviii. Kneller's drawing for Congreve's head (Witt Collection) is No. 46 (rep.). This account will no doubt be elaborated in the same author's forthcoming full-scale study of Kneller.

2. For a summary of Dryden's portraiture, see Piper, *Catalogue*, pp. 113–15, with earlier bibliography. Riley's painting (see *Burlington Magazine*, CIII (1961), 105 and rep.) is a very grand formal statement of Dryden in the poetic character, with a folio of Virgil's works and a bas-relief of the Muse.

3. For a summary of Prior's very rich portraiture, which includes works by Belle, Rigaud, and Coysevox besides those by British painters, see Piper, *Catalogue*, pp. 286–8, with bibliography. The Kneller and Belle portraits appeared side by side at the exhibition, *Cambridge Portraits*, Fitzwilliam Museum, Cambridge, 1978, Nos. 4 and 5 of the catalogue.

4. See J. W. Saunders, *The Profession of English Letters* (London and Toronto, 1964), pp. 130–5.

5. The source and strange development of Rowe's frontispiece was first observed by T. S. R. Boase (*Journal of the Warburg and Courtauld Institutes*, X (1947), 86). For Duchange's engraving, see Giles E. Dawson in *The Library*, 4th S., XVI (1936), 290–4; XVII (1937), 342–4.

6. See Piper, *Literary Portraits*, pp. 51–72.

7. W. K. Wimsatt, *The Portraits of Alexander Pope* (New Haven and London, 1965). Subsequent references here, apropos Pope's portraits, are mainly to this exhaustive work. Additional material is printed and reproduced in John Riely

and W. K. Wimsatt, 'A Supplement to the *Portraits of Alexander Pope*', in Wellek and Ribeiro, pp. 123–64. See also Morris R. Brownell, *Alexander Pope and the Arts of Georgian England* (Oxford, 1978).

8. Wimsatt, No. 1; Joseph Spence, *Observations, Anecdotes, etc.*, ed. J. M. Osborn (Oxford, 1966), I, p. 6 and rep.

9. Wimsatt, No. 2.

10. J. Prior, *Life of Edmund Malone* (London, 1860), pp. 428–9.

11. Wimsatt, No. 3. Brownell, op. cit., pp. 16–17, suggests the poet is shown distracted from the task of translating by the Muse (or Martha) putting away the book on the shelf. Alternatively, she may be taking it out.

12. Wimsatt, No. 5.

13. Tate Gallery, London, *Annual Report*, 1955–6, pp. 14–15, No. T. 56.

14. Wimsatt, No. 16.

15. Wimsatt, No. 62.

16. Wimsatt, No. 7.

17. Wimsatt, Nos. 7, 10–11.

18. Birmingham City Art Gallery. The print also appears in the first state of the engraving of Hogarth's subject, but alters in later states (see R. Paulson, *Hogarth's Graphic Works* (New Haven and London, 1965), I, pp. 174–6, No. 145).

19. Saunders, op. cit., 121–2, 135–8.

20. A. Pope, *Works*, ed. Elwin and Courthope, X (1888), pp. 139–40.

21. Wimsatt, No. 10.

22. Bromley-Davenport collection, Capesthorne; first published by J. F. Kerslake, *Burlington Magazine*, XCIX (1957), 24.

23. J. Richardson, *An Essay on the Theory of Painting* (1715), pp. 35–6.

24. Wimsatt, No. 9.

25. See especially Wimsatt, Nos. 19 to 48.

26. Wimsatt, Nos. 55 and 56; these entries are amplified by the recent discovery of a half-length version (now in the Paul Mellon Collection, Yale Center for British Art, New Haven): 'Pope in a mourning gown with a strange view of the garden to shew the obelisk as in memory to his mother's Death'. Riely and Wimsatt, op. cit., pp. 141–4 (as No. 56 X).

27. Wimsatt, No. 66.

28. Wimsatt, No. 64.

29. Wimsatt, No. 65. See also Nos. 15 and 16, Lady Burlington's earlier rough sketches of Pope seated pensive in his Twickenham grotto. William Kent, however, is now thought more likely to be responsible for these.

30. Wimsatt, No. 11.

31. For Roubiliac's busts, Wimsatt, Nos. 57–62.

32. James Prior, *Life of Edmund Malone* (1860), pp. 428–9.

33. James Boswell, *Portraits by Sir Joshua Reynolds*, ed. F. W. Hilles (New York, 1952), p. 24.

34. Wimsatt, No. 54. Oil portraits firmly ascribed to Richardson, Nos. 49–56.

35. Piper, *Literary Portraits*, pp. 65–6.

36. Piper, 'The Chesterfield House Library Portraits', in Wellek and Ribeiro, pp. 129–96.

37. The first reference to the south transept of Westminster Abbey as 'Poets' Corner' or, rather, 'the poetical Quarter', appears to be Addison's in *The Spectator* (No. 26), 1711. See also John Dart, *Westmonasterium* (London, n. d.); E. W. Brayley, *The History and Antiquities of the Abbey Church of St. Peter, Westminster* (1818–23), II, p. 266; N. Pevsner, *London – I* (Harmondsworth, 1962), p. 405. Pope's continuing involvement with the monuments and their

inscriptions, especially Shakespeare's, is described in Brownell, op. cit., Chapter 13.

38. For Scheemakers's Shakespeare, see Whinney, pp. 96–7; Piper, *Shakespeare*, pp. 20–5; Brownell, op. cit., pp. 354–6.

39. See J. L. Nevinson, 'Vandyke Dress', *Connoisseur*, CLVII (1964), 166–71. A. Ribeiro, 'Some Evidence of the Influence of the dress of the seventeenth century on costume in eighteenth-century Female Portraiture', *Burlington Magazine*, CXIX (1977), 834–40.

40. M. I. Webb, *Michael Rysbrack, Sculptor* (London, 1954), pp. 169–70; J. Douglas Stewart, in *Burlington Magazine*, CXX (1978), 215–22.

41. K. A. Esdaile, *The Life and Works of L. F. Roubiliac* (London, 1928), pl. xxvi b.

42. For Garrick, I have drawn especially on C. Deelman, *The Great Shakespeare Jubilee* (London, 1964).

43. W. T. Whitley, *Thomas Gainsborough* (London, 1915), pp. 66–9; E. K. Waterhouse, *Walpole Society*, XXXIII (1953), 47; 12, *Gainsborough* (London, 1958), p. 70, No. 304, and pl. 86; E. Wind, 'Humanitätsidee und heroisiertes Porträt in der Englischen Kultur des 18. Jahrhunderts', *Vorträge der Bibliothek Warburg, 1930–31*, pp. 211–12.

44. M. Webster, *Johann Zoffany* (National Portrait Gallery, London, 1977), p. 27, No. 12. Garrick's Temple is described and illustrated in *Country Life*, CXXX (1961), 201; it has since been thoroughly restored. A cast of the original statue was substituted when the marble went to the British Museum in 1822–3, but was given away in 1902.

45. K. A. Esdaile, *Life and Works of Roubiliac*, pp. 122–3.

46. The only photograph of B. Wilson's lost Shakespeare known to me is the indifferent print preserved in the Spielmann Shakespeare Archive in the Houghton Library at Harvard, reproduced here. It was signed and dated 1769: one of the books shown is titled *North's Plutarch*; a manuscript is headed *Henry 5th*. Though the setting is a fairly cosy study, the sitter (according to the *Public Advertiser* of 12 May 1769) is 'in the attitude of exclaiming "O for a Muse of Fire" '. A half-length rather similar in mood was at Warwick Castle.

47. Folger Shakespeare Library, Washington, DC, with a long inscription on its back recording the occasion.

48. For ceramic variations on Scheemakers's Shakespeare, see T. Friedman and T. Clifford, *The Man at Hyde Park Corner – Sculpture by John Cheere 1709–87* (Exhibition catalogue Temple Newsam, Leeds and Marble Hill, Twickenham, 1974). The Pope statuette is known from two versions, one in plaster (York Castle Museum, the Kirkleatham set) dated 1749, and a lead one in the Victoria and Albert Museum. Wimsatt, No. 61. 15/16; Friedman and Clifford, op. cit., No. 63.

CHAPTER 3

1. The most reliable discussion of Dr Johnson's portraiture is still that (by L. F. Powell) in Boswell's *Life of Johnson*, ed. G. B. Hill, rev. L. F. Powell (Oxford, 1934).

2. For Boothby, see B. Nicolson, *Joseph Wright of Derby* (London and New York, 1968), I, pp. 126–8, 182; II, pls. 219, 219a. Nicolson reproduces also Reynolds's straightforward head and shoulders of Boothby, painted only three years later, in 1784 (Detroit Institute of Arts).

3. Städel Institute of Art, Frankfurt am Main. Frequently reproduced, e.g. in E. Schaeffer, *Goethes Äussere Erscheinung* (Leipzig, 1914), pl. 27.

4. K. Garlick, *Sir Thomas Lawrence* (London, 1954), p. 58, pl. 110.

5. Engraved in mezzotint by Charles Turner, 1810. V & A, *Byron* Exhibition Catalogue, 1974, E.12.

6. e.g. National Portrait Gallery, London, No. 993.

7. C. K. Adams, *Catalogue of Pictures in the Garrick Club* (London, 1934), No. 13, as by B. Wilson, but almost certainly the painting of Powell and his family exhibited by J. H. Mortimer at the Society of Artists in 1768.

8. *John Flaxman, R.A.*, exhibition catalogue, ed. D. Bindman (Royal Academy, London, 1979), No. 117. Deposited in the Fitzwilliam Museum, Cambridge, 1980.

9. *The Diary of B. R. Haydon*, ed. W. B. Pope, III (Cambridge, Mass., 1963), pp. 293–4.

10. For the best summary of the monument's history, see M. H. Spielmann, *The Title-Page of the First Folio of Shakespeare's Plays* (London, 1924); also A. Wivell, *An Historical Account of the Monumental Bust of William Shakespeare* (1827).

11. See Vertue's drawing, drawn on the spot in 1737, of the chancel of the church, showing the monument as it was and still is (F. Simpson, in *Shakespeare Survey*, No. 5 (1952), pp. 55–7). Vertue had a cast of the head.

12. Most of the more important spurious portraits are discussed in Spielmann, *Conn.*

13. There are numerous derivatives from the 'Janssen' portrait; see Spielmann, *Conn.*, XXIV (1909), 231 ff.; XXV (1910), 105 ff.; XXVIII (1910), 151 ff.; XXXII (1912), 18 ff.

14. Sotheby's, 11 June 1947, lot 50 as 'Unknown man – said to be Shakespeare'; since unlocated. W. Brayley and J. Britten, *The Beauties of England and Wales*, (London, 1801–15) V, p. 679, record, 'Sir Thomas Overbury, half-length, in panel, by Cornelius Jansen' at the Ellenborough house, Southam Delabere. No portrait called Overbury surfaced at the Ellenborough sale of 1947.

15. R. L. Poole, *Catalogue of Portraits . . . Oxford*, I (Oxford, 1912), p. 30 and pl. IV (wrongly as by C. Johnson).

16. As illustrated on the cover of the Colour Supplement to the London *Observer*, 8 May 1977.

17. For Boydell's Gallery, see T. S. R. Boase, 'Illustrations of Shakespeare's Plays in the 17th and 18th centuries', *Journal of the Warburg and Courtauld Institutes*, X (1947), 83–103.

18. Fully analysed in M. D. George, *Catalogue of Political and Personal Satires* (British Museum, London, 1938), VI, pp. 637–9, and No. 7584.

19. Rep. E. K. Waterhouse, *Reynolds* (London, 1941), as of *c.*1781/2; now in the collection of Mrs Donald Hyde, Connecticut.

20. *George Romney*, Exhibition catalogue (Kenwood, London, 1961), Nos. 78, 79. There seem to be basically two designs, 'Nature unveiling the Infant Shakespeare' and 'The Infant Shakespeare nursed by Tragedy and Comedy'.

21. Gert Schiff, *Johann Heinrich Füssli* (Zürich and Munich, 1973), pp. 562–3, Nos. 1202–3. The original (which has been sold by King's College Hospital Medical School since Schiff wrote) is somewhat cut down: the original design is preserved in Moses Haughton's engraving.

22. C. F. Bell, *Annals of Thomas Banks* (Cambridge, 1938), pp. 73–4 and pl. XIV (engraving by B. Smith).

23. See W. Wells, *William Blake's Heads of the Poets* (Manchester City Art Gallery, n.d.), who discusses and reproduces the whole set.

24. Keynes, *Blake*, p. 139 and pl. 33.

25. Keynes, *Blake*, p. 135 and pl. 24.

26. Keynes, *Blake*, pp. 121–2 and pl. 7.

27. Keynes, *Blake*, p. 141 and pl. 36.
28. Keynes, *Blake*, p. 143 and pl. 39.
29. Keynes, *Blake*, p. 129 and pls. 20 a–b.
30. Keynes, *Blake*, pp. 131–3 and pls. 22 a–c.
31. Keynes, *Blake*, pp. 133–4 and pls. 23 a–d.
32. The Epstein and the Bacons do not come within Keynes's terms of reference. See R. Buckle, *Jacob Epstein Sculptor* (London, 1963), pp. 400–1, and J. Rothenstein and R. Alley, *Francis Bacon* (London, 1964), Nos. 92–4.
33. Most of the Keats portraits are discussed and reproduced in Parson, *Keats*. R. Gittings, *The Mask of Keats* (London, 1956), is concerned with the death mask.
34. Parson, *Keats*, pl. 38. Severn's comments are from his letter in the National Portrait Gallery archive (Reg. Pack, No 58). Severn also painted an impression of Keats listening to the nightingale – and one of 'Shelley composing his Prometheus Unbound amidst the Ruins of Rome'.
35. Parson, *Keats*, pl. 8.
36. The Vandyke was painted for Joseph Cottle: see his *Early Recollections Chiefly Relating to Samuel Taylor Coleridge in Bristol*, 1837. Coleridge's comments on Allston's portrait registered disapproval of his own face ('a FEEBLE unmanly face . . .') rather than the portrait. For Wordsworth Allston's was the only portrait of Coleridge that gave him 'the least pleasure', and Sara Coleridge thought it the best of him. For Coleridge's portraiture, see R. J. B. Walker's Regency catalogue, National Portrait Gallery (forthcoming).
37. Quoted by W. T. Whitley, *Art in England 1800–1820* (Cambridge, 1928), pp. 235–6.
38. Wordsworth's portraits are discussed and reproduced in great detail in Blanshard, *Wordsworth*, whence most of the quotations here are taken.
39. Blanshard, *Wordsworth*, pp. 53–60 and No. IX.
40. Blanshard, *Wordsworth*, pp. 89–91 and No. XXXVII.
41. Blanshard, *Wordsworth*, pp. 59–60 and No. XII.
42. Blanshard, *Wordsworth*, pp. 50–1 and No. V.
43. Blanshard, *Wordsworth*, pp. 61–4 and No. XIV.
44. Blanshard, *Wordsworth*, Nos. XXIV and LIV.
45. The catalogue by Anthony Burton and John Murdoch of the exhibition *Byron*, at the Victoria and Albert Museum, London, 1974, provides an extremely useful commentary, but is inadequately illustrated. Byron's *Letters and Journals*, ed. L. A. Marchand (London 1973–), Marchand's *Life of Byron* (3 vols., London, 1958; revised and shortened edition, London, 1971), and the works of Mrs Doris Langley Moore, especially *The Late Lord Byron* (London, 1961) and *Lord Byron – Accounts Rendered* (1974), are invaluable. I am greatly in Mr R. J. B. Walker's debt, for his generosity in allowing me to consult his entry for Byron in his forthcoming catalogue. Two articles by W. A. Shaw, 'The Authentic Portraits of Byron', *Connoisseur*, XXX (1911), 155 ff. and 251 ff., should be used with great caution.
46. Rep. e.g. R. Escholier, *Delacroix* (Paris, 1926), p. 50.
47. Cited by A. Bowness, *Courbet's Atelier du Peintre* (Newcastle-upon-Tyne University, 1972). The painting is in the Fabre Museum, Montpellier.
48. V & A, *Byron*, A. 41. For a full account, see O. Millar, *Later Georgian Pictures* (London, 1969), No. 1056.
49. Byron to John Murray, 12 October 1812 (*Famous in My Time*, ed. L. Marchand (London, 1973), pp. 224–5).
50. Byron to John Murray, 23 October 1812 (ibid., p. 254).
51. Quoted in V & A, *Byron*, C. 15.

52. V & A, *Byron*, H.8. (The National Portrait Gallery version; the original of Phillips's 'Albanian' version is certainly that now in HM Embassy, Athens, the three-quarter length reproduced here.) The relationship of Phillips's two designs (the head in each, 'cloaked' and 'Albanian', are virtually identical except for the moustache in the Albanian one) and the various versions of them are discussed at length in R. J. B. Walker's forthcoming National Portrait Gallery catalogue. The Newstead Abbey version of the cloaked design is the one that belonged to Byron himself.

53. Letter of about 1821, in G. S. Layard, *Sir Thomas Lawrence's Letter-Bag* (London, 1906), p. 95.

54. For Westall, see R. J. B. Walker's forthcoming National Portrait Gallery catalogue (he there notes that National Portrait Gallery, No. 1047 seems closer 'to the Ecce Homo at Langham Place' than to Byron). Exotic amongst the many engraved copies is a lithograph by Mavrin, Paris — *Lord Byron La Grèce Reconnaissante*. Westall's image became perhaps the most influential abroad: Ludwig Grimm's *Heine*, 1827, is identically posed, and was inscribed by Heine 'With a worn spirit and a cold heart I travel wearily through a cold world' (L. Untermeyer, *Heinrich Heine* (London, 1938), fp. and pp. 166—7). It seems to be a version of Westall's image that, with a bust of Beethoven, presides over Josef Dannhauser's archetypal gathering of romantic genius, 1840, about Liszt at the piano (Nationalgallerie, Berlin; Pl. 155).

55. V & A, *Byron*, J. 18 (Mrs Langley Moore's version). A. T. Storey, *James Holmes and John Varley* (London, 1894), p. 50. According to Marchand (*Life of Byron*, 1971 edition, p. 156), the portrait he sent to Frances Webster, 'dark and stern, even black as the mood in which my mind was scorching last July when I sat for it', was Holmes's, but the description seems to fit Sanders's better.

56. V & A, *Byron*, J. 19. The original drawing was sold at Sotheby's, 20 February 1968, lot 276. Widely known from H. Meyer's engraving of it for the *New Monthly Magazine*, 1 August 1815; Shelley owned an impression of this.

57. V & A, *Byron*, L. 1. Engraved in stipple by Scriven, 1820.

58. V & A, *Byron*, P. 4.

59. *New Monthly Magazine*, July 1832, pp. 5—6.

60. V & A, *Byron*, N.1. See R. J. B. Walker's forthcoming National Portrait Gallery catalogue; and especially Byron's letters to John Murray 16 May, 23 September, and 24 October 1822. For West's painting, John Club, 'The West Portrait of Byron', *Byron Journal*, no. 8 (1980), 22—30.

61. E. K. Sass, *Thorwaldsen's Portraetbuster* (Copenhagen, 1965), III, pp. 76—7. Thorwaldsen's account is first recorded by Hans Andersen.

62. V & A, *Byron*, R.16 (suggesting a partial derivation of the design from David's *Death of Marat*).

63. V & A, *Byron*, S. 22 (in the London art-trade (Roy Miles) in 1978). A good selection of Byronic memorials is recorded in V & A, *Byron*, Sections R (Death and Memorials) and S (Byron's Reputation in Europe).

64. V & A, *Byron*, R. 14 (Thorwaldsen's second model for the monument). H. W. Janson, 'Thorwaldsen and England', in *Bertel Thorwaldsen* (Cologne, 1977), pp. 107—28.

CHAPTER 4

1. W. Hazlitt, in 'Of Persons one would wish to have seen', first published in *New Monthly Magazine*, January 1826.

2. See Charles Lamb's account of the 'Bellows' portrait, in 1822 (*The Works of*

Charles and Mary Lamb, ed. E. V. Lucas (London, 1905), VII, pp. 573–4, with an editorial note on the portrait's history).

3. The colour structure was analysed by Miss Joyce Plesters at the National Gallery about 1964.

4. The Flower portrait is discussed in Spielmann, *The Title-Page of the First Folio of Shakespeare's Plays* (London, 1924), pp. 37–8.

5. Anthony Burgess, *Shakespeare* (Penguin edition, 1972).

6. S. Schoenbaum, *William Shakespeare: A Documentary Life* (Oxford, 1965); id., *Shakespeare's Lives* (Oxford and New York, 1970), pp. 464–73 (a brisk summary of some of the more celebrated doubtful portraits).

7. Spielmann, *Conn.*, 1–4.

8. T. Kay, *The Story of the 'Grafton' Portrait of William Shakespeare* (London, 1914); Spielmann, *Conn.*, 3; J. Dover Wilson, *The Essential Shakespeare* (Cambridge, 1932), fp. and Chap. 1 *passim*.

9. L. Hotson, *Shakespeare by Hilliard* (London, 1977). See S. Schoenbaum, in the *Times Literary Supplement*, 28 October 1977, p. 1261.

10. For Spenser's portraiture, see D. Piper in Wellek and Ribeiro, pp. 186–7 and pl. 2.

11. *The Portraits, Prints and Writings of John Milton* (exhibition catalogue, Christ's College, Cambridge, 1908), p. 34, No. 22 and rep.

12. See *The Diary of A. C. Benson*, ed. P. Lubbock (London, n.d.), p. 160: 9 February 1907, 'Every time I look at it the beautiful soft eye of the charming boy seems to regard me reproachfully for giving him away; but he ought to be in Trinity.'

13. In the Stratford-upon-Avon Royal Shakespeare Theatre Gallery. Dated 1857, and exhibited RA 1857 as 'A Sculptor's Workshop, Stratford-upon-Avon, 1617'.

14. Sold in Helmut Tenner's rooms, Heidelberg, 3 November 1960, lot 421.

15. F. M. Hueffer, *Ford Madox Brown* (London, 1896), pp. 57–8: 'Carefully collated from the different known portraits . . . the attempt to supply the want of a credible likeness of our national poet . . .' Brown's *Chaucer* was certainly based closely on Rossetti (Hueffer, p. 67).

16. Verbal information from Sir Roland Penrose, 1964.

17. A representative (though far from exhaustive) selection of Staffordshire Shakespeares is reproduced in P. D. Gordon Pugh, *Staffordshire Portrait Figures* (London, 1970), H. 574–5.

18. See R. Ferriday, 'Free standing and civic', in *Studio International*, CLXXXIV (1972), 42–3. Trelawny claimed that Belt's statue did not 'in the remotest degree represent Byron either in face or figure' (quoted by P. W. White and R. Gloucester, *On Public View* (London, 1971), p. 155 and rep.). Lord Edward Gleichen thought it possibly '*the* very worst statue in London' (*London's Open-Air Statuary* (London, 1928), pp. 61–2 and rep.).

19. Thackeray noted a Shakespeare Head inn-sign in Paris in 1841 (*Works*, 1898 ed., XIII, pp. 361–2). For Fournier's statue, with reproduction, see Y. Bizardel, 'Les Statues parisiennes fondues sous l'occupation', in *Gazette des Beaux-Arts*, 2 March 1974, pp. 129–52.

20. Two versions are in the British Museum. See *John Flaxman R. A.*, ed. D. Bindman (exhibition catalogue, Royal Academy, London, 1979), No. 7 and rep.

21. Tate Gallery, RA, 1856. Described by Ruskin as 'faultless and wonderful'. See R. Treble, *Great Victorian Pictures* (Arts Council Exhibition catalogue, 1978), pp. 83, 84.

22. For the Curran portrait of Shelley, see E. Dowden, *Life of Shelley* (London,

1886), II, p. 265; S. Marshall, *Life and Letters of Mary Wollstonecraft Shelley* (London, 1889), II, p. 137; R. Holmes, *Shelley, The Pursuit* (London, 1974), pp. 512, 516–17. Both the Curran portrait and Clint's copy of it are in the National Portrait Gallery (see R. J. B Walker's forthcoming catalogue, *Regency Portraits*).

23. For the two Shelley monuments, see F. Haskell, 'The Shelley Memorial', *Oxford Art Journal* (Oxford, 1978), I, pp. 3–8. The Christchurch monument was originally intended for St. Peter's, Bournemouth, where Shelley's heart is buried (N. Pevsner and D. Lloyd, *Hampshire* (Harmondsworth, 1967), p. 177). Thomas Love Peacock (in *Fraser's Magazine*, June 1858) thought that all portraits wanted the 'true outline of Shelley's features, and, above all . . . their true expression'. He thought a self-portrait of 'Antonio Leisman' (Eismann) at Florence was more like Shelley than any authentic portrait (but Peacock knew it only from an engraving).

24. Ingres, Louvre; (Petit Palais, Ingres exhibition catalogue, Paris, 1967–8, No. 141); R. Rosenblum, *Jean-Auguste-Dominique Ingres* (London, 1967), pp. 130–3; H. Honour, *Romanticism* (London, 1979), pp. 52–5 and 337. In reproduction, Shakespeare's head tends to get chopped in half. In the revised design which Ingres planned about 1840 he was omitted altogether.

25. Ashmolean Museum, Oxford. The full-scale finished version of the formal design is in Sydney, Australia, a smaller replica in the Tate Gallery. Mary Bennett, *Ford Madox Brown 1821–1893* (exhibition catalogue, Liverpool, 1964), Nos. 11 and 12.

26. For my purposes, H. Tennyson, *Alfred Lord Tennyson: a Memoir* (London, 1897) and P. Henderson, *Tennyson, Poet and Prophet* (London, 1978) have been the most illuminating biographical accounts. R. B. Martin's *Tennyson: the Unquiet Heart* (Oxford, 1980) appeared too late for me to profit from it and its excellent illustrations. An extensive summary of the portraiture is given by Ormond, with many reproductions.

27. e.g. National Portrait Gallery, No. 2460. Ormond, I, pp. 448–9.

28. Woolner's versions of Tennyson are fully described and documented in Ormond, I, pp. 450–3.

29. National Portrait Gallery, 3940. Ormond I, p. 450.

30. Listed by Ormond, I, p. 454; V. Surtees, *The Paintings and Drawings of Dante Gabriel Rossetti* (Oxford, 1971), No. 526. The prime original, given to Browning, was presented by Mrs Donald Hyde to Columbia University Library, NY. Rossetti made two replicas.

31. Quoted by Henderson, op. cit., p. 201.

32. Watts's portraits of Tennyson are listed and illustrated with bibliography, by Ormond, I, pp. 447–8.

33. N. Hawthorne, *English Notebooks*, entry for 30 July 1857.

34. H. Gernsheim, *Julia Margaret Cameron* (London, 1948), pp. 82–3, pls. 7, 52, and 22. Gernsheim dates the full-face photograph as *c.*1867, the 'Dirty Monk' as 1865, the other (pl. 52) as June 1869.

35. See Ormond, I, p. 452 apropos National Portrait Gallery, No. 1667. The original marble is in Adelaide, South Australia.

36. For Browning's portraits and their bibliography, see Ormond, I, pp. 70–6. According to Ormond, the most comprehensive account is G. E. Wilson, *Robert Browning's Portraits, Photographs and Other Likenesses and their Makers*, ed. A. J. Armstrong, *Baylor Bulletin*, XLVI (December 1943), No. 4. The National Portrait Gallery possesses a cast of the clasped hands of Robert and Elizabeth Browning.

37. Christopher Hassall, *Rupert Brooke* (London, 1964): for Schell's photographs,

see pp. 389–91; for the Brooke 'myth', especially Chapter XIV, 'Man into Marble'. Schell's own account, 'The Story of a Photograph', was printed in *The Bookman* (New York), August 1926, pp. 688–90.

38. Siegfried Sassoon, *Siegfried's Journey 1916–20* (London, 1945), pp. 49–51 and fp.

39. The fullest survey of Yeats's portraiture seems to have been contained in the exhibition at Manchester and Dublin in 1961, on the catalogue of which (*W. B. Yeats, Images of a Poet* – referred to below as 'Yeats, 1961') I have drawn extensively.

40. Yeats, 1961 lists a number of portraits by J. B. Yeats.

41. For John's portraits of Yeats, see M. Holroyd, *Augustus John*, I (London, 1974), pp. 259–63, and Yeats, 1961, Nos. 28–33, 35, 43, and pls. 4–6.

42. Yeats, 1961, Nos. 24, 24a, and pl. 3.

43. Yeats, 1961, No. 26 as location unknown. Fp. to Vol. III of the *Collected Works*, 1908; an Emery Walker positive on glass of the original is in the National Portrait Gallery archive.

44. Yeats, 1961, No. 34 as location unknown.

45. Quoted in Yeats, 1961, p. 13.

46. Yeats, 1961, No. 48 and fp.

47. W. Michel, *Wyndham Lewis, Paintings and Drawings* (London, 1971), No. P80 (and No. P79, a smaller version). Michel (p. 132) claims it as 'a profound painting', with the poet 'rather than offering an appearance for the benefit of posterity, contemplating himself and the realm of his imagination'. Eliot said he would be quite pleased to be known to posterity through it. Lewis's later portrait of Eliot (Magdalene College, Cambridge; Michel No. P124) was painted in 1949 when the artist was almost blind. Versions of two portraits, 1960–2, by Sir Gerald Kelly were sold in the sale of his studio contents, Christie's, 8 February 1980, lots 234, 235 (rep. in the catalogue).

48. National Portrait Gallery, No 4467. See the NPG *Annual Report 1965–6*, pp. 33–4 (and p. 18 for Epstein's bust of Eliot, NPG No. 4440).

49. L. Gordon, *Eliot's Early Years* (Oxford and New York, 1977), p. 75.

50. G. M. A. Richter, *The Portraits of the Greeks* (London, 1965), I, pp. 70–2.

51. H. Ward and W. Roberts, *Romney* (London, 1904), I, p. 110 (rep.); II, p. 141.

52. For Elizabeth Barrett Browning's portraits, see Ormond I, pp. 67–70.

53. V. Surtees, *The Paintings and Drawings of Dante Gabriel Rossetti*, I, Nos. 420–33.

54. E. Salter, *Edith Sitwell* (London, 1979), is a pictorial biography, with very rich (though far from exhaustive) illustration. A great deal of information is to be found in J. Pearson, *Façades* (London, 1978). Victoria Glendinning's excellent *A Unicorn among Lions* (London, 1981) appeared too late for me to able to profit from it.

55. F. R. Leavis, *Aspects of Modern Poetry* (London, 1932), p. 73.

56. E. Sitwell, *Alexander Pope* (London, 1930), p. 10.

57. Quoted by J. Pearson, *Façades*, p. 392.

58. Pearson, *Façades*, p. 140. Her collection of works by Tchelitchew was sold at Sotheby's, 13 December 1961, the catalogue with a foreword by her, and two portraits, including the remarkable wire and wax mask, reproduced.

59. M. Chamot, D. Farr, and M. Butlin, *The Modern British paintings, drawings and sculpture* (Tate Gallery, London, 1964), I, pp. 264–5, pl. V.

60. Tate Gallery; W. Michel, *Wyndham Lewis, Paintings and Drawings*, No. P36. The drawings are Nos. 485–8 and 592.

61. C. Beaton, *The Book of Beauty* (London, 1930), p. 36.

62. Formerly in the collection of Laurence Whistler; sold Sotheby's, 20 December 1967, lot 80.

63. 'Squares and Oblongs', in *Poets at Work*, ed. C. D. Abbott (New York, 1948), p. 176.

64. Vernon Scannell, *A Proper Gentleman* (London, 1977), p. 13.

65. By Eric Kennington; unveiled by J. M. Barrie in 1931.

66. See M. Holroyd, *Augustus John*, II (London, 1975), pp. 95, 227 (n. 538).

Acknowledgements

The text is revised and expanded from the Clark Lectures delivered at Cambridge in 1978, and my thanks must go to the Master and Fellows of Trinity College, who, firstly, commissioned this rather unorthodox addition to the roll of Clark Lectures, and secondly, and most generously, made a handsome grant towards costs of the reproductions in the published version.

The theme has been developed from work in the National Portrait Gallery from many years back, and I have touched on it in different ways in earlier publications (see Notes, p. 201). It depends to a very large extent on the unique archive of the National Portrait Gallery, and on the work of my predecessors and former colleagues there. I am especially grateful for help on this occasion from Miss Sarah Wimbush in the Guthrie Room at the Gallery. On specialized aspects I am indebted to the late W. K. Wimsatt, with whom I spent many happy hours in pursuit of Alexander Pope in the early 1960s; to the late J. M. Osborn; to Mr Richard Walker, Consultant Extraordinary at the National Portrait Gallery, for help on subjects in his research for his Regency catalogue; to Sir Geoffrey Keynes, my former Chairman at the National Portrait Gallery.

I thank all those, individuals and institutions, as credited in the List of Illustrations, who have granted me permission to reproduce portraits in their care, and apologize to those few owners whom I was unable to trace.

I owe a great debt again to Chris Dale-Green, endlessly patient in typing and re-typing, and to Susan le Roux and Fran Holdsworth at the Press for their sympathetic and imaginative guidance of the text into print.

The book is dedicated to the memory of Tim Munby, formerly Librarian at King's College, Cambridge, the imaginative generosity of whose concern for all scholars was unsurpassed.

Index of Names

Text references in ordinary type: plate references in bold type